SUCCESSFUL BUSINESS BORROWING

SUCCESSFUL BUSINESS BORROWING

How to Plan and
Negotiate a Loan

KENNETH W. SPARKS

WALKER AND COMPANY

NEW YORK

First published in the United States of America
in 1986 by the Walker Publishing Company, Inc.

Published simultaneously in Canada by John Wiley & Sons
Canada, Limited, Rexdale, Ontario.

Library of Congress Cataloging-in-Publication Data

Sparks, Kenneth W.
    Successful business borrowing.

    Includes index.
    1. Credit. 2. Bank loans. I. Title.
HG3751.S65 1986   658.1'5224   86-13135
ISBN 0-8027-0902-8

Printed in the United States of America

10 9 8 7 6 5 4 3 2 1

To Pearson Hunt, professor of finance and banking, emeritus, at the Harvard Business School. He will barely remember his student of thirty years ago, but I remember him and his talents as a teacher and kindness as a person very well. By this dedication I thank him—and through him all the teachers in schools and mentors in business who have given me so much.

CONTENTS

FOREWORD

In this book the terms "banker," "loan officer," and "account officer" are used interchangeably. They all mean simply the person at the bank or other credit institution who has primary responsibility for your account. I will refer to that person randomly as male or female. This is not to pretend that banking is not a male-dominated industry. It is. However, most banks, and all the quality banks, now actively recruit, train, and promote women for supervisory and executive positions. As a result of these programs the typical female loan officer is as capable as her male colleague. In recent years, in my experience, she tends to be more capable.

The credit institution you are to deal with will usually be called your "bank" or "lender." This is merely a convenience. Your creditor may be a conventional commercial bank, a savings and loan association, a leasing company, an industrial finance house, or your father-in-law. The same principles of credit apply to all of them, and no one source of credit is necessarily any "better" than another.

Throughout this book I have tried to use correct financial terminology. My terminology, however, is not consistent: often the same event or document will be given a different name. This reflects actual practice in commercial finance where many terms are used loosely and interchangeably. Exposure to a wide vocabulary of these terms here will help the reader when he meets them in the real world of credit.

INTRODUCTION

This book creates a level playing field for the businessman or -woman who wants to borrow money. Most business owners or executives are intimidated by financial institutions—typically, the marble-halled bank—and are not aware of what they can win through knowing the ropes. Very few even know how to prepare and present an effective credit application, let alone how to negotiate with Mr. Moneybags.

Using more than twenty-five years of experience, both as a lender and as a borrower, the author shows the reader the mechanics, the rules of the game, the opportunities, and the pitfalls. He explains how to line up potential sources of credit, how to judge loan officers, how to play one source of credit against another, when to grab an offer with both hands, and when to back off. And, most important, with this knowledge the reader will have *confidence*, an essential asset in any negotiation.

The text is illustrated not with pictures but with real-life examples of how borrowers have won or lost when the chips were down, and why. Some of the stories are humorous; not one is frivolous; each proves an important point.

Throughout the book there are tables and accounting schedules to help the reader translate the text into calculations and practical financial statements. The Appendices contain advanced material for readers who wish to go into specialized areas. Great care is taken to inform first-time borrowers and yet to include (and explain) tactics, strategy, concepts, and terminology useful to more experienced businessmen.

Who can use this book? Most of the 17 million businesses that file U.S. tax returns annually *plus* the 600,000 entrepreneurs who start up new businesses every year. Only a tiny fraction of these enterprises are large enough to have a financial executive devoted full-time to raising borrowed money and maintaining relations with the financial community. Most firms, in fact, seldom negotiate a new line of credit more than once a year. Yet this "part-time" activity is too important to be done casually, and if done carelessly can create nightmares, even insolvency. Thus this book steps in to provide the information required to borrow money like a full-time professional does—knowledgeably.

Fortunately the basic principles of credit and credit negotiation are fairly constant, regardless of the size of the borrower. The reader need not be concerned that his enterprise is too large, too small, or too different. A great mansion uses the same kind of electricity as a tiny cottage. Whether we are talking about hundreds of kilowatts or hundreds of thousands, the principles of electricity are the same.

Also, whether we will be talking about thousands of dollars or millions, the dollars, like the electricity, are only of value when they are used to produce something of value, be it widgets or a hot meal. Hence the chapters to follow emphasize the basics of developing and refining profitable uses for credit, and they show how this preparatory work is used to win the credit itself.

After the credit has been approved, further chapters explain how to achieve another goal that is even more important, and that is *maintaining a successful credit relationship*. A business dependent on credit too often neglects this vital—and continuing—factor in its financial future.

SUCCESSFUL
BUSINESS
BORROWING

1.

THE PROJECT: WHY DO YOU WANT THE MONEY?

There is an old recipe for rabbit stew which begins, "First you catch the rabbit." When you borrow money you, too, will need a "rabbit" to get started: a concrete and limited purpose that the borrowed funds will help accomplish. We will call this purpose the "project," not because this word is a precise term in banking (it is not), but because it is common in finance, flexible and easy for the layman to grasp. It can accommodate any discrete economic activity, from restocking your shelves to retraining your sales force to building the Grand Coulee Dam.

Without a project you will not get money from the bank unless you are very rich. IBM and the United States Treasury can borrow from the banks without a project. You and I cannot. While this will be self-evident to most readers, to others it will not. A recent client of mine had applied to five banks for a loan "to start a business." He got five quick rejections. He wanted to know what he had done wrong. Well, at least he specified "to start a business," which, if you think about it, is better than "general purposes."

1

Defining the Project Precisely

The project should be as specific and accurate as possible. Consider these alternatives for the same use of funds:

1. to finance higher sales; or
2. to help finance work-in-process on four specialized radio transmitters already ordered by RCA Corporation.

Alternative 2. shows the bank that: a) the applicant is seeking only a portion of the funds required; b) he knows exactly where the requirement is going to impact his working capital; c) he is building against a firm order rather than on hopes of a sale; and d) the customer is a knowledgeable and highly creditworthy buyer. These facts would probably emerge anyway during interviews or elsewhere in the loan application. The point is that alternative 2. shows the lender immediately that the applicant knows precisely why he needs the funds and how he will use them. Moreover, this is the kind of project a bank loves to finance. The loan is self-liquidating; that is, the economic activity that created the need for funds will itself generate the cash to repay the loan.

Understanding Why You Need the Funds

We have gotten ahead of ourselves and must retrace our steps. The first and most important value of the clearly defined project is not to impress the bank, but to determine *why* you need the money. Sometimes the reason is stark: a valuable shipment has been lost in transit, and you need a bridging loan pending receipt of the insurance proceeds. Other cases may be deceptive. Your inventories are growing and can no longer be financed from receivables collections. Is this a project you should finance with borrowed funds? Maybe.

Consider these possibilities:

1. Your inventory is not growing, only the inventory values on your books are. The difference is pilferage.

2. Both your inventory and sales are increasing, but your gross margins are shrinking, thereby eating up the extra cash required to support an increasing level of sales.

3. That portion of your inventory which supplies 80% of your sales has shrunk from 40% of total stocks to 15%. Your inventory is out of balance and parts of it are excessive.

In these unhealthy—and quite common—examples, the need is not a new loan. On the contrary, a loan would help conceal and exacerbate the problem. The need is management action on inventories.

This book is not about general management, so I must cut short this digression (which could be carried on into receivables, capital equipment, and so on). Nevertheless, the point must be reemphasized: you have to understand exactly why you need the financing. If you do not analyze the requirement and determine the "ultimate why," you may suffer terrible consequences.

Do not expect your banker to do this work for you. It is not his job, and usually he is not equipped to do it. An outstanding account officer, especially one with extensive experience in your industry, will sometimes identify even the most mysterious and secret problems in your business. Do not count on this.

For many would-be borrowers, now is the moment of truth. If you misidentify the reason you need financing, you might make the worst (and possibly the last) mistake of your business career. If not part of a plan to correct underlying problems, a new loan is more likely to increase than to reduce your need for cash; not immediately, of course, but quite soon, and then with a vengeance.

To the many readers—perhaps a majority—to whom these warnings do not *now* apply: you have not wasted your time. Remember this page. Reread it whenever you apply for a new loan. Your time will come.

Multipurpose Requirements
Some borrowers will be seeking funds to accomplish several projects. No problem. Each one should be broken out and considered independently, both as to its justification and, as explained later, its economic consequences. Make every effort, here and later, to keep different projects conceptually and financially separate. Do not include the refurbishing of executive offices in the cost of a new rolling mill. This is only a form of self-deception, and it will make subsequent efforts to "prioritize" competing demands for scarce capital misleading and more difficult.

Try to keep the number of projects down to a manageable few— three or four, maximum. More than that will confuse both you and your lender. Stick to those that show the greatest economic return and in other respects are the most necessary and tangible. Lower-priority projects can be financed from your own funds; they are not the best candidates for borrowed monies. (I realize that in one sense this distinction is illusory, since in terms of dollars all purposes are fungible. As a practical matter, however, the bank likes to think its money is going into hard tools, not soft draperies.)

Planning for an Adequate Lead Time

This is a good place to warn about a completely different subject: having adequate time to get the best financing possible. There are many variables which can affect how long the whole process will take, but we can talk "order of magnitude." Say, one month to analyze your project and prepare your application for financing; another month for lender review and negotiations; and a third month to accommodate revised proposals, unexpected demands, and other delays. Particularly if you are going out to borrow for the first time, I would recommend you plan on a minimum period of three months. Four would be better.

Most lenders will decide on a small credit request, say $20,000, in a week or two; if approved, the availability of funds will be only a fortnight thence. Fine, assuming your credit and collateral are beyond question. Unless you are experienced, however, you cannot know that this will be the case. Most candidate borrowers should expect a longer period. If we are talking about preparation time, extensive negotiations, getting the best possible deal, and several candidate lenders, then several months, not weeks, will be the norm.

Make no irrevocable commitments during this period, unless implementation of the project does not hinge on the financing sought. Instead of signing a lease, pay for an option on a lease, the cost of the option to be recovered if you exercise it. Make down payments for equipment only if they are refundable. Too many things can go wrong to take the chance of losing monies committed. Further, if you are forced to proceed before a looming deadline, you will have lost flexibility. You might be squeezed into compromises that more time would have rendered unnecessary.

2.

WHAT ARE THE ECONOMICS OF YOUR PROJECT?

Having defined why you want a loan, you quantify the economics of your project over time. By "economics" we do not mean here the impact on the Gross National Product; we just mean the financial consequences of your project for: 1. the project itself; 2. the lender; and 3. your overall business (assuming your project is part of, rather than your entire, business).

Forecast Financial Statements

The first step is to take the project itself. The uses to which you put the loan or leased assets will have economic consequences over time. You forecast these consequences as sales, increased receivables, expenditures on plant and equipment, accounts payable, and so on, in what are called "pro forma financial statements." They are also variously called prospective results, forecasts, budgets, business plans, feasibility studies, or prospectuses. Do not concern yourself with these different terms. You call them whatever your loan officer calls them. In this book we will refer to them by all these names, just to keep your vocabulary broad and flexible.

There are common and generally acceptable formats for these forecasts, and the terminology is widely understood. Lenders can cope with variations from industry to industry. The three basic formats are:

1. the Profit and Loss Statement (abbreviated as P&L and sometimes called the Statement of Earnings, the Income Statement, or the Statement of Income and Expenditure)

2. the Balance Sheet (abbreviated as B/S and sometimes called the Statement of Assets and Liabilities, or the Statement of Financial Condition)

3. the Cash Flow (also called the Flow of Funds, Statement of Receipts and Expenditures, and several other names)

Examples of all these financial statements will appear later. Forecasts can use the same formats and terminology as historical statements of financial results. Indeed, you should use the same formats and terms so that historical and forecast statements can be readily compared.

Mechanics of Preparation

All financial statements, whether past or future, final or preliminary, should be clearly identified as such. Since forecasts are often revised several times, it helps to note in the corner of the schedule the date of preparation or revision. In my experience this is more than helpful; it is essential for tracking back the final numbers. When several persons are involved in preparing forecasts, the preparer's initials should appear on each worksheet. Underlying workpapers should be attached or kept in a file referenced on the worksheet.

You may wonder why such "housekeeping trivia" are discussed. The answer is, the better you understand how your numbers were put together, the better you can explain them and justify them to the loan officer. You want to show a detailed and quick grasp of your business, to be "on top" of your numbers, not confused by them. No one can appear confident with numbers arising from sloppy, undated, and conflicting financial schedules. If your loan request is sizable and your business complex, backup papers will be required during discussions with your lender. Do not go to the opposite extreme of typing them up on vellum; it is wasteful and looks suspicious.

Let us return to the project forecasts. If you cannot do them yourself or with your own staff, then make a best effort and ask your outside accountant to help complete them. If your accountant is part of your permanent staff and he cannot do the job, stop until he learns how or until you get a new accountant. Preparing project forecasts is a learning experience for small companies particularly, but as will be explained later, it is an integral part of the management tools of financial budgeting, analysis, and control. If you cannot prepare forecasts on a level of sophistication commensurate with the size of the loan you are seeking, you probably will not get the loan. If you do get it, your control of the proceeds will be inadequate.

In case preparing the forecast is beyond your skills and you do not have an accountant to help, you can find assistance in the *Yellow Pages* under Management Consultants and Accountants. Even then, you yourself should do as much as you can—for example, the sales and manning forecasts and the schedule of capital expenditures. The more you leave to outsiders, the more uncertain your grasp of the numbers will be. After your preliminary work, look over the specialist's shoulder while she completes the job. Insist on understanding each step—to the extent that next time you can do it unassisted. Another source of help (and this one costs nothing) is your local library. Even a small library will have several books on basic accounting, budgeting, and business planning; these will include detailed explanations and examples.

You may have wondered why the project forecasts, if not the same as the forecasts for your entire business, should be broken out and shown separately. The reason is that the project, if it is worth investing in, should stand on its own two feet. If you bury the project in your overall business, it might be a poor investment without your realizing. By the same token, you might have a great project subsidizing an awful business, and you would not want that concealed in consolidated statements, either. Hence the economics of the project are broken out and subjected to independent scrutiny. No separate corporation is required. You just "create" with paper and pencil a new profit center to see how it works. (The desirability of forming a new legal entity for the project will be discussed in Chapter 4.)

A Concrete Example

Let us take the sale of the four radio transmitters to RCA Corporation as an example of how the three key forecasts might look. Although the cycle of this project takes place within a (roughly) known period of time, we do not look at the whole period only. It is broken down into time periods, so we can see clearly what is happening *inside* the whole cycle. These smaller periods can be years, months, weeks, or any combination thereof. The example does not say which, and this is to remind you that you have to select the periods that best reveal what is actually happening "inside" your project.

The oft-quoted adage that you can drown in a lake with an average depth of two feet illustrates perfectly why this time-division is necessary. The key figure you want from the time-period analysis is your maximum cash requirement. If the time periods you select miss that maximum moment, your loan will be too small and you will be in trouble. This is what your forecast should be designed to avoid.

In the following forecasts several assumptions were made to simplify the accounting. The most critical was that the day after the end of the time periods 1 and 2, fabrication is completed, the finished product shipped, and payment received. This eliminates any accounts

FORECAST PROFIT & LOSS STATEMENTS (in $000)*				
	Period 1	*Period 2*	*Period 3*	*Cumulative totals*
Sales	—	300	900	1,200
Cost of goods sold				
Direct labor	—	45	135	180
Direct materials	—	39	117	156
Depreciation	—	60	180	240
Factory overhead	—	42	126	168
Total cost of goods sold	—	186	558	744
Gross profit	—	114	342	456
Expenses				
Marketing, general, & administrative	48	48	48	144
Interest	15	33	—	48
Total expenses	63	81	48	192
Profit before tax	(63)	33	294	264
Income taxes at 50%[†]	(31)	16	147	132
Profit after tax	(32)	17	147	132
*Includes contingencies of	9.6	15.0	38.1	62.7

*Includes contingencies of
[†]For convenience, assumed to be reduced or paid when booked.
Contingency analysis explained in Chapter 7.

FORECAST BALANCE SHEETS (in $000)*

	End of:	Period 1	Period 2	Period 3
Cash		15	36	405
Accounts receivable		—	—	—
Work-in-process		186	558	—
Total current assets		201	594	405
Tools and dies		240	240	240
Less cumulative depreciation		(60)	(240)	(240)
Total assets		381	594	405
Bank notes payable		110	336	—
Supplier accounts payable		30	—	—
Total current liabilities		140	336	—
Owner advances		273	273	273
Cumulative net profit (loss)		(32)	(15)	132
Total liabilities & equity		381	594	405

FORECAST CASH FLOWS (in $000)*

	Period 1	Period 2	Period 3	Cumulative totals
Sources of funds				
Owner advances	273	—	—	273
Receivable collections	—	300	900	1,200
Bank financing	110	226	(336)	—
Suppliers payable	30	(30)	—	—
Total sources	413	496	˙564	1,473
Uses of funds				
Direct labor	45	135	—	180
Direct materials	39	117	—	156
Tools & dies	240	—	—	240
Factory overhead	42	126	—	168
Marketing, etc. expense	48	48	48	144
Interest payments	15	33	—	48
Income taxes	(31)	16	147	132
Total uses	398	475	195	1,068
Net change in cash	15	21	369	405

*Includes contingencies per Profit & Loss Statements

receivable, and it picks up the instant of peak requirement for financing work-in-process. The forecasts also assumed the project was part of an existing business, so the owners could use the loss in the first period to reduce their total taxes. The P&L and Cash Flow schedules show a fourth column, Cumulative Totals. These generally are not included in formal presentations, but I think they are useful summaries—a kind of overview of the project. They also help to identify arithmetic and conceptual errors in the earlier time periods. Add up the numbers horizontally, and the resulting totals should check out vertically.

The forecasts just presented assume combined local, state, and federal income taxes at a rate of 50%. This is only for convenience: your rates will vary according to your circumstance. Your forecasts should show them on a separate line, since they represent significant outflows. Projects which generate zero tax liability or even negative tax cash flows are more complicated; they might require a separate subschedule. Sales taxes, employment-related taxes, and property taxes are included in Sales, Direct Labor, Factory Overhead, or General & Administrative Expense, as appropriate.

After you have prepared your three basic financial forecasts, some comments are in order. Do they all tie into each other and are they internally consistent on their own? In short, do the numbers add up? These questions involve accounting and mechanical problems we do not have time to discuss here, but the numbers must be correct if your forecasts are to be credible. Surprisingly often, arithmetic discrepancies result from conceptual and logical shortcomings. If you do not resolve these discrepancies, you risk overlooking more serious problems.

The Key Elements of Credibility

The preparation of financial forecasts, like historical financial statements, assumes some competence in accounting or access to accounting expertise. This book does not provide either. It does insist that your forecasts be credible, and it will try to make them credible, no matter what your credentials as an accountant.

The four key elements of credibility, for both you and your lender, are:

1. Can you achieve the forecast sales?
2. Are your forecast costs reasonable?

3. Will you get the project done on time?

4. Will you generate the cash to repay the loan?

Lawsuits from environmentalists or resulting from falling aircraft can disrupt the best-laid plans, but lenders, unless they are dealing with very large sums, do not look at loan applications with these worries in mind. (They do want you to be properly insured, and you should have or prepare to have suitable coverage before you apply.) Lenders will look at the four key elements.

Attainable Sales

You will need to write up your market position and prospects: competition, location, historical dollar and unit volumes, pricing pressures and opportunities, product life cycle, market volatility, and so on. If you are unsure of the factors affecting your sales forecasts, you will have to do some market research to ensure that you have covered all the bases. The project sales forecast should discuss each major factor under a separate heading. Your opinions should be subdued, or better, left out. If the facts cannot speak for themselves, your case is weak. Industry-wide statistics, local traffic patterns, household income distribution, and demographics are more convincing than unsubstantiated expectations.

In my example of the sale of transmitters to RCA, I neatly avoided the all-important question of future sales. Unless your project neatly fits my example, you cannot.

Containable Costs

To the extent you are vulnerable to cost overruns, you should get firm quotations from subcontractors and suppliers that will ensure that your costs are known and fixed. If these suppliers are not reliable and financially sound, the bank will not be impressed, nor should you.

Dependable Timing

This risk deals with delays, how you plan to avoid them and, when they happen, how you will cope with them. Manufacturing delays are obvious—for example, late delivery of a key component. Delays in market acceptance of your product are much more difficult to plan against. Standby plans might provide for product repackaging, redefinition of the market, or new promotional strategies. The financial counterpart of this analysis of potential delays should be a loan request or cash reserve large enough to accommodate these possible setbacks.

A list of *all* the events that could conceivably delay the success of your project would be endless and not practical. For discussion in your loan application, pick the two or three most important and most likely; explain your planned countermeasures. For yourself, a longer list, perhaps fifteen events, should be developed, and you should have a contingency plan for each. Some delays, such as getting planning permission, may be impossible to counter with alternative actions. In these cases, work out a rough estimate of the costs and consequences. Make sure your contingency fund is large enough to absorb them.

Adequate Cash Generation

Our sample Cash Flow showed a substantial cash residual after the bank loan has been paid off: $405,000. With a cushion that size, repayment of the loan is well protected. A surplus of only $25,000 in our project would be clearly insufficient. Too many things can go wrong for either borrower or lender to rely on such a small margin. The appropriate size of the margin will depend largely on the risks inherent in the project, and these should be analyzed and quantified as discussed above.

If you own or have access to a personal or microcomputer with a financial spreadsheet program such as Crunch or Lotus 1-2-3, you may wish to produce your forecasts that way. This is particularly true if your existing accounts are already computerized and/or if the project is complex and has many variables. A financial computer program is especially helpful if you want to prepare "what if" scenarios and follow their effects among the three basic statements. At the opposite extreme, an unusually simple project (such as our example) can be worked up by hand faster than it would take using a computer. Anyone who has tried using a computer to balance his personal checking account will understand what I mean.

3.

A DETACHED REVIEW

Pleasant surprise! You have completed most of the hard and dirty work required, and not for the bank. You want it for yourself. Now you can sit back and survey your project as if you were Andrew Carnegie considering a new steel mill.

Add in a few contingencies and problems. Cut sales by 10%. Assume your largest customer defects to the competition, your landlord refuses to renew your lease, your warehouse supervisor resigns. No falling aircraft, just the ordinary events that do and will happen to any business. They need not—and they will not—all happen at once.

Weigh up these problems and balance them. Think about them and what they might result in (perhaps getting a better lease elsewhere). This *really* is what the most sophisticated investors do after the weeks of preparatory dog's work are over. They sit back and try to restore the objectivity they surrendered during their intense involvement with developing the project.

You do the same, and if you still like the numbers and the project, proceed to the next chapter.

4.

SELECTING A LEGAL ENTITY

Satisfied with the economics of your project, you now should consider the best place to plant and nurture it. Specifically, what is the most suitable legal entity to own it and finance it? Sometimes the company that owns the project will be different from the company that finances it, and this choice of ownership will almost always impact the financing of the project. You should not approach a potential lender without having given this question some hard thought. You need *not* make a firm and final decision. You *should* be aware of the choices and how they are likely to affect the terms and conditions of the financing.

Examples of Choices

Suppose a department store wanted to close out its line of costume jewelry and replace that merchandise with expensive watches and precious stones. This is a new project, and the increased investment in the new inventory would be a sensible candidate for new bank financing. Unless we assumed several unlikely and complicated conditions, there would be no reason for the store to consider having the new merchandise owned by any other entity than the store itself.

At the opposite pole might be a manufacturing concern which needs a new, $250,000 numerically controlled machine tool. Because of heavy investment in other new equipment, this firm has excess, unused tax credits. Further, its debt is already excessive. In this case the answer probably is to have a leasing company buy and retain ownership of the new machine. Because the leasing company can use the tax benefits, it can charge the user less for the machine than it would cost the user to own it. Also, the lease entails no large "up-front" requirement for borrowed funds to finance the purchase (though restrictive covenants in existing loan agreements could be a problem).

Remember that the ownership and transfer of tax benefits through leasing can become a highly technical subject. If certain procedures and criteria are not observed correctly, the intended benefits could be disallowed by the Internal Revenue Service. Unless the transaction is small and straightforward, such as leasing a delivery van or copying machine, you should get expert advice. Assuming you are dealing with a highly reputable company, such as Greyhound Leasing, advice on the legal and tax aspects of the lease can be had for nothing from the lessor. (The financial aspects are another matter; see Appendix C.)

Here is another candidate for project ownership by a party other than the user. Suppose the owner of a personal computer store needs more space, wants to build new premises for his business, and has the funds to finance the down payment. Although the personal computer business is booming, he feels that because of accelerating technological change, his is a high-risk industry. So he forms a new company to own the new building, and his computer sales company rents the premises. If the computer business later collapses, he still owns the real estate and can relet it to a new tenant.

Construction companies traditionally form a new legal entity for each major contract, and they try to finance each such project independently. This practice is standard and accepted. Some companies, however, alienate their assets deviously through separate corporations in order to frustrate collection by unsuspecting creditors. ABC Company may appear very prosperous—with a huge warehouse and a fleet of trucks all labeled "ABC Company"—but they may all belong to someone else.

Inescapable Trade-Offs When Alienating Assets

These and many other variations on the ownership of the project can materially affect your ability to finance it with borrowed funds—or to finance it at all. Clearly, any increase you obtain in the security of your assets through alienation (ownership by a third party) can only be gained at the expense of banks and other creditors. Transfers of advantage in security (assets available for seizure in the event of nonpayment) will cause compensating changes in the availability and cost of credit.

It is an inescapable trade-off. Hence the ownership of your new project cannot be decided without considering the effect on the creditworthiness and credibility of the entities involved. Fraudulent or excessive alienation of assets may fool—for a time—your smaller suppliers, but it will not fool a bank or major supplier. An effort to protect yourself beyond customary standards will cost you your good name, and you will have given up more than you have gained.

After these warnings I should emphasize that there often are perfectly sound reasons to insulate your assets from creditors, to give them to your brother-in-law. Be candid with your lender as to why you did it. Say, "I realize that this reduces the assets supporting this loan request, but I had important reasons for structuring the business this way." Then explain your reasons. If you acted intelligently and honestly, that only shows your business good sense and integrity. The worst the bank can do is insist that the alienated assets be included in the pledged collateral. These assets do not have to be transferred to the ownership of the borrowing entity; they only have to be accessible to the creditor.

5.

SELECTING TARGET LENDERS

Now you have a profitable project; that is, a use for borrowed funds that you can present to a bank. Before preparing your application, however, you should begin your search for a list of target lenders. Then continue both efforts simultaneously to save time. The first step in targeting lenders is to collect information.

Gathering Background Information

Nose around. If you are just getting started, ask your neighbors and local shopkeepers. If you are already in business, ask your suppliers, your major customers, and your business colleagues. To do this with useful results, you have to be rather hard-nosed. In old-fashioned banking, it was not done, and some opprobrium may linger in your community. However, to get the best leads, this is the way to do it. You have to be blunt with your informant. What rate of interest does First National Bank charge you? Do you pay compensating balances? If so, how much and how are they calculated? (We will discuss these and other banking terms in later chapters.)

Throughout this book, by the way, I usually refer to the lender as a bank. This is only for convenience, a shorthand way of referring to any source of credit, whether commercial bank, savings and loan association, finance company, leasing company, financing arm of an equipment supplier, or equity investor who also provides debt capital. Whatever their names, their money is the same color. They all want roughly the same information and will use similar criteria in evaluating you and your proposal. Generalizations can be made about their lending practices, but these will never be so useful to you as a factual comparison of the specific terms they offer.

Along with facts and opinions about the banks, you should get names and evaluations of the local loan officers. Do not be put off by a single horror story about a particular account officer or lender. Some loan officers are not competent, and all banks mishandle some loans, just as some auto mechanics are not competent, and all automobile manufacturers produce an occasional lemon. Unless the unfavorable information is widespread, absorb it, but do not act on it. At this point you are working on probabilities, and one instance may prove nothing. Sometimes .derogatory "information" is wildly biased and out of date.

For some enterprises a key source of information may be a major existing or potential supplier. Aggressive suppliers, particularly of capital equipment, know that restricted cash and/or credit often is a limitation on new sales. Hence they develop credit sources, contacts, in-house capabilities, and other means to help prospects pay for new purchases. Since these suppliers may service scores of firms in your area, they may be well placed to know which local sources of credit are hungry and flexible. If your supplier is personally not well informed, ask her to check with her headquarters and see what she can learn.

The Initial Interview

After the preparatory work just described, you should contact someone for an initial interview. If you feel comfortable with a referral, write the loan officer recommended. If not, write a higher officer in the bank subsidiary.* In either case, write a brief letter, stating that you would like an appointment with a loan officer for a preliminary discussion. Describe your specific project briefly, with no superlatives or adjectives. State the amount you plan to borrow and indicate, if

---

*Look the name up in *Polk's World Bank Directory* at your library. Try to find the local executive responsible for your geographic area. Writing to the Chairman of the Board will only annoy him and everyone below him.

you can do so honestly, that this will become part of a larger relationship.

If your addressee does not reply within two weeks, phone him, referring to your letter. If he is out, refer to the letter and ask to be called back. If there is no answer after another week, write to a higher level in the bank or forget that institution. My advice is to forget the bank that does not reply to letters and phone calls. Most of us live within striking distance of a dozen potential sources of credit. The minority that are too busy, disorganized, or discourteous to answer your inquiries are best discarded. Pay no attention if these same rejected lenders are advertising widely for new customers; you are interested in performance, not advertisements.

At your preliminary meeting do not give out any write-ups or financial schedules. Give a brief oral summary of your existing business or business background, the new project, the additional sales it will generate, and a rough indication of the size and duration of the credit sought. Mention two specific facts to prove you have researched your project—for example: Arthur D. Little's study of demand for lightweight automotive subassemblies concluded the market will grow 35% a year, compounded; my chief engineer, who has an advanced degree in materials engineering, has proved that we can make this strut for 40% less than the competition.

State that your project figures are not final, but that you have analyzed them carefully and they are in the ballpark. On the basis of this information, you would like to know who the loan officer would be and her title, what documents you should include with your loan application (e.g., prior tax returns), any further information required, and what terms the bank might be expected to offer on a loan of this type. Be sure to get a copy of the bank's application form and any written material it has on bank lending policy. Some, not most, banks will give you a printed statement of their lending criteria and requirements.

When, during this preliminary interview, the lender asks what collateral you have to pledge, reply that you would prefer to postpone that subject until the need arises: according to your calculations the project will stand on its own and generate more than sufficient funds to repay the loan. If pressed, state that you doubt collateral will be required, but if it is, then you would be prepared to consider providing it. Do not be drawn into a discussion of existing debts, mortgages, personal assets, etc. You are not applying for a loan at this time, you are seeking information. The reasons for this posture are: 1) to avoid giving the impression that even without negotiating the conditions, you have conceded the need for collateral; and 2) to avoid the bank's rejecting your approach out of hand because it thinks you have insufficient collateral or none.

During the initial interview you should also get a rough idea of the timing and mechanics of the bank's approval process. Ask whether a loan of the size you are considering would be approved at the branch or whether approval at a higher level would be required. How long does a decision typically take? The lender may refuse to be specific and say, "Well, each case is different," or answer with some similar evasion. Do not be put off. Explain that you are not trying to pin the bank down, you merely want an indication for your own planning purposes. Are we talking days, weeks, or months? Faced with this question, no loan officer will claim he can give no indication at all.

During these interviews you should take notes, beginning a separate file on each credit source. The key points arising in all subsequent phone calls and meetings should be added to the file, with careful note of the exact time, place, and persons involved. This practice has proved of great value to me several ways, not the least was having a record to support my understanding of an oral agreement when the account officer had none. Another good practice is to get back immediately to your lender for clarification when, a day later, you feel unsure as to what was said, agreed, or meant. *Never* ignore an uneasy feeling in such cases.

One Candidate Lender or Several

At this point you want to have three or four candidate lenders who seem friendly, receptive to your project. If one lender was unqualifiedly enthusiastic, and the rapport with the loan officer was outstanding, you should consider a compromise. Forgo the advantage of being able to compare competing offers and proceed with the one lender you like so much. You might pay a point more in interest (1% per annum more on the principal balance outstanding), but if the loan is for a small amount, the savings in your time and hassle may be worth it.

On the other hand, that open-armed, welcoming bank may, down the road, insist on a general lien on all your business and personal assets—a condition another bank might not require. You have not burned your bridges, but when you return to your second choices, your resumed effort might be "tainted" by failure to reach agreement with the first bank.

In short, when you hawk a deal sequentially, all but the first customer might smell soiled goods. When you hawk it to all simultaneously, you have an auction, and the whole process takes much less time. If the first potential lender lures you into a dependent relationship with glowing prospects, your freedom of action will be compromised. There are few rules of thumb here; you must use your judgment. The most sophisticated and largest borrowers sometimes get it wrong.

A correction is called for here. No responsible bank—and very, very few are not responsible—will "lure" you into a dependent relationship on purpose. What happens is that the negotiations deepen and lengthen, without either party intending it, until both have invested so much time in the result that neither is willing to give up. Or, more likely, the bank is quite willing to give up, but you are not because you have committed yourself to an impractical goal with that particular bank. In this latter case, you may offer greater and greater concessions in pursuit of an unobtainable goal. Worse, you may finally get the loan—in exchange for costly and onerous terms.

One of the few rules of thumb is that the larger the loan (let us say over $100,000), the more you should incline to multiple bidders. Another is, the more complex the financing, the easier and faster it is to work it out with one cooperative bank. The best illustration of this is the United States Treasury. It always auctions its domestic short-term debt because the instruments are simple and standard, and the volume is huge.

A Diversity of Financial Institutions

Your target lenders should be as different as possible in market orientation and size. This conclusion contradicts common sense in most purchasing decisions: ordinarily you seek equally qualified suppliers with specialized capabilities. In finance this is true on a large scale, as in the auction of United States Treasury debt. On a smaller scale, the market can be so diverse, aggressive, and innovative that it is best to forget traditional categories for sources of credit.

For example, a French bank, at my suggestion, flew a team to Chandler, Arizona, to review a seasonal loan requirement of only $500,000. No international business was involved. This bank is only one of many foreign-owned banks seeking out such remote opportunities in the United States. Of course they would rather lend tens of millions at one shot to a name like IBM. IBM, however, can issue its own debt; the little company in Arizona cannot. The new financial institution (or an old one entering new markets) has to search farther afield for new business and to be more flexible. Hence these potential lenders are as much candidates for your trade as the traditional commercial bank on Main Street.

As part of a national policy to remove unnecessary federal regulation, in the early 1980s Congress passed legislation permitting savings banks and savings and loan associations to make commercial loans. Previously they were confined largely to real estate mortgages. Most of the larger institutions affected by this deregulation have set up departments to cater to their new market, the business borrower. Include one on your target list.

The General Electric Credit Corporation originally financed only sales of GE products. Now most of its loans are made to finance assets having no relation to its parent's business. Its minimum loan for working capital is approximately $2 million. It will lease equipment with a value as low as $100,000, pick up the tax benefits, and possibly leave you with a better profit and cash flow than a bank loan would. Your local bank, however, if it is in the leasing market, may be competitive, especially on smaller sums.

The larger consumer finance companies, such as those advertising on television, now have divisions to serve business clients—for example, Household Finance Corporation. They tend to be more expensive than banks; they are also more flexible. The phrase "finance company" might give rise in the minds of older readers to Depression Era images of heartless, usurious moneylenders. Such stereotypes no longer apply. The modern finance company catering to businesses is no less respectable as a source of credit than its commercial banking counterpart.

The local *Yellow Pages* is an excellent starting point for leads. Look under the headings for Banks, Leasing, and Financing. If your area has a *Business to Business Yellow Pages*, be sure to use that directory rather than the regular *Yellow Pages*, the latter is oriented to consumers. In my region the *Business to Business* directory, under the heading Financing, has more than eight times as many column inches as the consumer *Yellow Pages*. If you are approaching this stone cold, I suggest that for finance companies you select names you recognize such as Armco (a subsidiary of the steel company), Greyhound, ITT, Pitney Bowes, and affiliates of major banks. Picking a name at random, such as XYZ Funding Corporation, may connect you with a broker, bucket-shop operator, or usurer. These all have a place in the system, or they would not survive; but they should not be among your first choices.

Until you exhaust every possibility of credit from well-known sources such as mentioned above, do not consider approaching firms advertising loans at absurd rates of interest. In early 1984, for example, the *New York Times* carried this ad: "8.9% Mortgages, Bank Loans, Corporate & Start-ups, Call . . ." At the time the ad appeared the advertiser could have invested in medium-term U.S. Treasury bonds yielding 12.5% *with zero risk and administrative expense!* Clearly this was a highly deceptive "come-on," designed to attract the unwary.

In most cases a variety of financial institutions will generate a better offer than will the same number of commercial banks. Similar banks servicing similar markets will, not surprisingly, offer similar terms, sometimes even identical terms. (This is seldom the result of collusion or market fixing: given nearly identical variables in the same economic equations, the solutions are bound to be nearly identical.) Further, different credit markets have different cycles of expansion and retrenchment. The expanding sector will price more aggressively. Giant corporations track these sectoral changes and the lending appetites of individual institutions within them. This is not possible for the smaller firm, so the safest strategy is to approach widely different markets. Assuming you want to finance equipment or other depreciable assets, a reasonable mix might be a commercial bank, a finance company, a leasing company, and a savings and loan association or savings bank.

Because the industry is changing so rapidly and so much depends on individual cases, few generalizations about large banks vs. small banks are useful. Firms having many local offices receiving payments and businesses requiring export credit services should favor larger banks with branch networks and foreign trade departments. This is obvious. (If you already have a banking relationship and are considering changing, you should review now Chapter 14, When and Whether to Change Your Bank.)

For a fuller discussion of the recent history of the finance industry and "asset-based" lending in particular, please see Appendix D. This appendix also provides a detailed comparison of the typical asset-based loan with a conventional commercial bank credit.

6.

PREPARING THE LOAN APPLICATION— PRELIMINARY COMMENTS

During your preliminary interview the loan officer may have said, "Mr. Elder, my bank knows of your company, and we think very highly of it. For a loan the size you are requesting the bank can almost certainly go forward simply on the basis of your most recent audited financial statements." In this and similar situations you may wish to proceed without a full-blown loan application—a lot of work to no purpose. I do suggest, however, that you read through the material here about the loan application. Most of it will be of interest to any borrower; some of it will be of value whether or not you make a full presentation; and much of it ties in with subsequent chapters.

While the core of your application is the presentation of the financial statements of your business and the new project (Chapter 8), the application should include a discussion of these figures. This written review will give the loan officer and the bank's credit committee a "feel" for your business, how you see your business, and how you run your business. Almost all credit decisions are in part qualitative judgments, so you want to satisfy the bank's interest not only in your numbers but in your ability and credibility as a manager.

The Application as a Selling Document

This brings us to a major purpose of the loan application: it is a *selling* document, a sales tool. Its purpose is to sell your project, your business, and yourself to the bank. A high degree of confidence in these will often overcome a bank's reluctance to lend against a weak balance sheet. Conversely, a strong balance sheet may not overcome a poor opinion of management.

Selecting a Format

Almost all *consumer* credits require filling out a printed application form. The degree of detail required in the application is largely a function of the amount of the credit for which you are applying. Most *commercial* lenders do not have standard application forms.

The distinction between consumer and commercial credit is important. The extension of consumer or personal credit is controlled by, and the borrower is protected by, very rigid and complex governmental regulation. Your particular lender probably has in-house policies that impose additional restrictions. Commercial lending, on the other hand, makes the assumption that the loan applicant is a knowledgeable businessperson who understands the risks involved; hence this kind of lending is not subject to anywhere near the same degree of regulation. Consumer credits are almost invariably extended on the basis of simple formulae that are applied to key figures submitted in the application—for example, income level, years on the job, and home ownership. Commercial credits are extended on the basis of a case-by-case evaluation of the merits and risks of each application. The criteria used are much more liberal and flexible.

Make sure you do not apply at the wrong window, or your business application may be rejected as not meeting the criteria of a consumer loan. For most applicants this confusion is unlikely, but for some it has happened. A recent case I came across involved a businesswoman who wanted to add an office extension to her home. Her application was rejected out of hand at the consumer loan window: she did not pass the formulae tests. As a commercial applicant she would have succeeded easily.

Let us return to your commercial loan application. The reason few lenders have a standard form to fill out is that every business sector uses different formats for its financial statements, reflecting the unique economics of its business activities. Even firms within the same sector will often use different formats to separate out or to ignore what is or is not of importance to them. Lenders generally accept the utility of this diversity and do not require a standardized presentation. Besides, the bank's credit analyst usually does not work directly on your financial statements. She extracts key data, reformats them, subjects the results to ratio tests, and studies them for trends.

In the event your lender does have printed forms, resist using them or reformatting your figures to fit them. First of all, your statements will highlight or reveal key facts better than the bank's format, which is a general one developed to accommodate any kind of business. Second, you probably store your historical results, budgets, and forecasts in a computer. They are all comparable and can be printed out and photocopied at negligible cost in time or money. Reformatting is time-consuming and apt to introduce arithmetic errors and inconsistent definitions of accounting categories. Finally, your bank will require periodical financial statements and possibly regular updates of your forecasts. Imagine the labor involved to reformat quarterly reports and forecasts for the next six years! Chances are at some point you will have a new accountant who does not even know how to do it.

Internal Goals and External Commitments

Although convenient, using your internal budgets and forecasts in your loan application can be hazardous. Budgets, business plans, five-year forecasts, and similar projections prepared by management ordinarily have several purposes, not all of them relevant to your loan application. The principal purpose of your sales budget, for example, may be to set the highest possible goals for your marketing staff. These goals, however, are probably higher than you realistically expect them to achieve, even under optimum conditions. Now assume less than optimum conditions (adverse weather, delayed product introduction, etc.), and you will have to ratchet down your expectations another 5% or 10%.

This lower sales volume is what you should forecast in your loan application because: 1) it is more defensible; and 2) when you achieve it or exceed it, your credibility will be enhanced. A forecast compound annual sales growth of 40% may look good to you; in most cases it will appear foolish to your lender, evidence of inexperience and gullibility. A growth rate of 15%, well-supported with facts and cogent argument, is more convincing and, once accomplished or exceeded, more impressive than any 40% forecast.

The same comments apply to planned reductions in costs of materials, improvements in productivity, reductions in marketing expense relative to sales volume, collections of overdue receivables, and so on. An excellent check on whether you have been too optimistic is to look at your bottom line: does it show a profit "too good to be true"? If it does, it probably is.

Over the past 29 years I have studied many hundreds of business plans, budgets, and new venture proposals and then tracked the actual results. The rule of thumb that emerged was: the more extravagantly lucrative the forecast profit, the more certain the enterprise to fail— not to fail to make the profit only, but to fail, period. Any lender in business for more than a few years has learned the same lesson.

Why is "super growth" so implausible? Because ours is a market economy with generally free entry to new competitors. Above-average profits, and particularly super profits, will attract more competition until profits in that sector or subsector approximate the average for that level of risk. Economics One at your County College. Do not try to fight Economics One in your loan application unless you have 1) an impregnable patent position, or 2) the only license to pump oil in the Oklahoma Panhandle.

These comments notwithstanding, you can still show very large "one-off" increases in sales or profits if you have a one-off event to justify them, an event the new loan might help make possible. An expansion of sales floor area to promote a popular and exclusive line of goods, additional production machinery to break a bottleneck in capacity, and a cost-reducing new printing press are all investments that can arguably, even demonstrably, generate markedly higher levels of sales and/or profits. You may have already proven this in your study of the economics of the project (Chapter 2).

Be careful not to replicate blindly a one-off event in subsequent forecast accounting periods. By definition, the event is nonrecurring. Even if the extra revenue or expense reduction is expected to continue beyond one year, the usual course of competition and growth in overhead will almost certainly dilute the initial advantage. If you install a fabulous new press this year, the printer across the street will install it next year. Even if he doesn't, repairs and maintenance after your warranty has expired will reduce your profits.

7.

THE REQUIREMENTS OF A SUCCESSFUL APPLICATION

This chapter will deal with what your application should include and how to present your material. Concurrently it will review what the bank will need to approve your loan from a credit point of view. After all, the most elegant and informative application in the world will be approved only if the proposal is creditworthy.

The Three Basic Tests for Creditworthiness

The three basic tests for creditworthiness are:

1. adequate owner's equity and unencumbered assets;
2. sufficient earning power and/or cash flow to repay the loan, with a generous margin of safety; and
3. confidence in the business ability and integrity of the management and owners.

A few readers may argue with these tests because they know that some financial institutions will, considering test 1., lend to an entrepreneur so famous and adept that his record and name alone can command credit; or, considering test 2., lend to a near-bankrupt enterprise if the value of the collateral is sufficient; or, considering test 3., lend to Al Capone if the interest rate is rich enough. I can only agree that such exceptions do occur, and they are always interesting, often fascinating. Yet they *are* exceptions, and unless you can meet some very rare criteria, you will have to qualify for my three basic tests.

Test 1. Equity and Unencumbered Assets

The entrepreneur starting a new business often finds the requirement of adequate equity the biggest hurdle, so we will devote some time to the start-up venture before moving on to businesses in general. Since some comments apply in either case, you should read this section even if you are not starting from scratch.

There is no secret or magic source of equity capital for the new venture. The computer genius may be able to find his angel because he comes from a select circle of brilliant engineers and promoters, but very few of us work at MIT or count as close friends the millionaires of Silicon Valley. Most of you will have to raise your equity capital from your own resources, your personal contacts, friends, and relations. If you cannot, you will not get even a tiny bank loan. You may be able to *lease* equipment from suppliers—delivery vans, kitchen equipment, machine tools, even furniture and fixtures. In the event these assets are sufficient to get you under way, and you want to take the chance, then try it. But you will have the worst possible capital structure: no equity base and no cushion to accommodate a bad turn of events.

Your equity need not be entirely in cash. Part of it can be contributed, indirectly, by pledging the equity in your home or some other asset as collateral against the debt financing required. Generally speaking, however, this form of indirect equity will not carry as much weight as cash or other assets contributed directly to your business. Lenders always prefer to see that the enterprise can stand alone as creditworthy, even though they may require personal guarantees and liens on external assets as well. No lender wants to foreclose on your home; she wants your *business* to repay the credit extended.

Debt and equity are, in a sense, two sides of the same coin, the coin being the capital structure of your business. No credit analyst will ignore your equity base (shareholder/owner funds), and the smaller it is in relation to the credit sought, the more difficult it will be to get that credit on favorable terms—if at all.

Also, if you start off with an undercapitalized business, you dramatically increase the likelihood of failure. The best opportunities and management in the world cannot compensate for unforeseeable events that suddenly create losses and rapid cash outflows. An adequate equity base can. The United States Small Business Administration has estimated that one-third of all business failures can be attributed to an insufficient equity base.

It is not possible to state in absolute amounts or percentages what an adequate equity base should be for a new enterprise. There are too many variables. Even giving illustrative examples for a variety of businesses would be misleading, since so many cases are unique.

You can, however, make comparisons with existing businesses in your industry subsector and in your approximate size group. These comparisons will not give you a definitive answer, though they will give you a feeling for what a lender expects to see in your sort of enterprise.

For a relatively small business, refer to *Financial Studies of the Small Business*, published by Financial Research Associates, Inc. My library has a copy; yours should, too. In Appendix B in my book you can examine sample pages from that book for two different industries, both broken down by size of firm. (By the way, when I speak of an "industry," I do not mean only a category of manufacturing. The word is used as economists use it, to describe any natural group or subgroup of similar economic activity—for example: Retail Trade or Family Clothing Stores; Metal Fabrication or Aluminum Extrusion.)

Larger businesses (those with annual sales over $1 million) can also research what other firms are doing by identifying competitors that have shares traded on the stock exchanges. These competitors may be located anywhere in the country. You can write to the company secretary for its Annual Report and Form 10K (which usually includes all the financial information in the Annual Report plus much additional detail). These reports will disclose in full the firm's capital structure and may provide you with much other useful information. You can find summary information on these same businesses by looking them up in Moody's or Standard and Poor's basic reference books in any library.

Please remember that when using these reference sources you will be looking at *established companies*. Since you are planning a new business or a major expansion, you will probably have large start-up and other expenses before you reach their level of ongoing, profitable activity.

Suppose, for example, that Competitor "X" shows a debt of $500,000 and a net worth of $1 million; you consider "X" a reasonable model for your firm; and you would like to plan your own debt + equity capital structure on that basis, a 1:2 debt/equity ratio. Now suppose that your new project is forecast to lose $250,000 before it begins to make a profit. If you start out with the capital structure assumed, you will soon be up to $750,000 in debt and down to $750,000 in equity, a ratio of 1:1. This may not be acceptable to your lender. You may have to increase your initial level of equity to wind up at the desired position.

The other side of our two-faced coin is that lenders are not rigid, nor are they dummies. They realize that any new enterprise or major expansion of an existing one will probably lose money for at least the first few months. A carefully anticipated loss in profits and/or outflow of cash during this period is normal, and you should argue that it is temporary, even inevitable. In this case there may be no need to increase your equity investment just to accommodate a short-lived deficiency. However, you *will* have to convince your lender that the shortfall is temporary. Your lender will not accept a debt/equity relationship that is permanently out of line or stands a good chance of becoming so.

Here are some further observations on the subject of equity:

1. You may have read about "leveraged buy-outs" where the new owner does not put up any cash; the seller and the banks finance 100% of the purchase price. Where is the equity? It is in the value of the assets financed and their future earning power. Properly arranged, the business is worth substantially more than the loans extended to purchase it. The difference between the buy-out price and the real value constitutes a "cushion" of equity (even if it does not show up on the books) available for depletion in the event of losses; and this cushion serves to protect the lenders from loss. Very likely there will be another hidden source of equity in the form of guarantees or the pledge of assets extraneous to the business. But one way or another, if there is not sufficient equity, hidden or overt, the bank will not extend a loan.

2. If the banks you approach all say your equity is insufficient to support the amount you want to borrow, then it is. They have

the money, and they are more experienced than you. Sometimes this is not black and white, as we will review later in Chapter 10 on negotiations. Nonetheless, as a rule, a firm "not enough" from three lenders on this point should be accepted as fact. You have to raise more equity.

3. The banks, contrary to the common saying, are not there to lend you an umbrella only on a sunny day. Their business is to make a profit by lending their money at risk, just as your business is to make a much larger profit by putting your equity capital and time at risk. The banks do not look for risk-free loans because such loans yield almost nothing over their own cost of funds. Paradoxically, they need the risk in order to make money. At the same time, they sensibly try to minimize that risk. If you put yourself in their shoes, you will see what they are trying to do.

4. A good banker will tell you the truth about your need for additional equity. Unfortunately, some lenders will not do that. They will fob you off the pseudo-reasons for rejecting your application: "Right now, our portfolio for this kind of business is full," or "We would like to see one more year of growth in sales and earnings before moving forward on this." These evasions are difficult to recognize for what they are. To smoke them out, ask, "If I put $25,000 more of my own money into the business, would that make a difference?" Even if you do not have that money to put up, your offer might elicit an honest answer. Or you can ask, "If the security of your loan is a problem, how much additional equity and/or collateral would make you feel comfortable?" If the answer is 250% of the loan required, either you have a very shaky business or your loan officer is not willing to tell you what his real objection is. Assuming your discussions have gotten this far, you should be able to tell which answer applies.

With the benefit of this background, we can return to the first test to qualify for a loan: adequate owner's equity and unencumbered security or collateral in the assets of the business. Although adequate equity would usually also mean sufficient unencumbered assets, this is not necessarily the case. Suppose an entrepreneur contributes $50,000 in cash to his equity to buy inventory; then he gets $50,000 in credit from a supplier to buy another $50,000 of inventory; to induce the supplier to extend the credit, he unwisely gives the supplier a lien on the entire resulting inventory worth $100,000. In this simple example, the original equity contribution may have been enough to support a small commercial loan. The owner, however, has "converted" his equity into inventory and then given contingent ownership of that asset to the supplier. The value represented by the equity (the first $50,000 of inventory) is no longer accessible to the bank, and there is no basis for a loan.

We can also imagine the reverse case: unencumbered assets and inadequate equity. Suppose our entrepreneur puts up $1,000 in equity and then induces trade suppliers to ship him $100,000 of goods on open lines of credit, unsecured. Although the bank could, in theory, make a perfectly safe loan of $25,000 to this business, using the inventory as secured collateral, it almost certainly will not. There is so little equity to absorb a loss, the business is not creditworthy. Remember that lenders do not like foreclosures, even when they are fully protected. The delays, nuisance expenses, and legal costs will mean a net loss on the transaction. Further, they have forgone the profit they could have made lending the same money to a sound business. Even less does a lender wish to seize a debtor's home which has been put up as collateral. It may take months or years to get the debtor out, and it makes for poor community publicity.

Now go back to the forecast financial statements we used in Chapter 2 to establish the economics of a project. In this case the balance sheet shows an infusion of owner's funds sufficient to create a sound basis for a new loan, and there are no preexisting or planned pledges of assets to dilute the bank's security interests. In this case we have satisfied the first test. The absolute numbers and the ratios, by the way, are only an illustrative case, conservatively biased, to support my claim that here we have a bankable proposition.

For readers who wonder why, in this discussion of equity, I have not used the magic words "venture capital," the reason is simple: the principal subject of this book is raising borrowed money, not equity finance. (Chapter 19 contains a review of venture capital as a source of equity.)

Earning Power and Cash Flow

Our second test of creditworthiness is sufficient earning power and/or cash flow to repay the loan, with a generous margin for safety. Key concepts here are "earning power" (or accounting profits) and "cash flow." A rapidly growing business can show rocketing profits but run out of money because it is expanding faster than its cash resources allow. When its cash runs out, the firm is insolvent. It cannot pay its bills, regardless of how real and lucrative its profits were or how much owner's equity was available as a cushion. These cases are not infrequent. They are particularly sad, since usually such businesses will have to be liquidated for a fraction of their values as going concerns. Typically the owner's equity will be wiped out. He will have lost everything, whereas he could have survived and prospered had he settled for a lower rate of growth.

At the opposite extreme is a business which is actually losing money, according to its book profits, but is generating a strong positive cash flow. An enterprise engaged in an orderly liquidation of valuable real estate might fit this description, and under these circumstances a lender might find it a very attractive client.

So your lender will look at both your earning power or book profits *and* your cash flow. This is why you present both a Profit & Loss Statement and a Cash Flow.

Our project forecasts in Chapter 2 illustrate a case where both the profits and cash flow are positive, obviously the most attractive case from a lender's point of view. If both forecasts are negative, your chances of raising a loan are slim, and this would be prima facie evidence of a poor investment (unless you are into some complex tax scam, but that is another matter). If one indicator is negative and the other positive, you may have a sound investment or you may not. You have to analyze what is going on "inside and behind" the numbers. Then you can explain to the bank why what appears at first glance to be unfavorable is actually a desirable and planned development.

The final element of the second test is "a generous margin of safety." The easiest definition of "generous" in this context is "more than enough." Translating this definition into hard numbers may not be easy. If the only variable in the success of your project is an engineering calculation of physical tolerances, you may be able to quantify with high accuracy your expected scrap or reject rate. Supposing all the other costs and expenses and the price are fixed, we might need a margin of safety of only 10% in this example.

If the key variable is market acceptance of a new and faddish consumer product, subjective judgment may be your only guide. In this case your margin of safety will have to be very large, perhaps 100% or 200%. Most business assessments require both quantitative and qualitative assessments, and the margins of safety will fall well within the extreme examples just described.

The most important object here is not to get that margin of safety exactly right, which is impossible, but to spend a lot of time defining it and trying to quantify it. When you have done that, you will have a much better understanding of your project, and you will be able to convince your loan officer that your numbers are not just plucked out of the air. You will have confidence, and you will instill confidence in others.

Occasionally there are some guidelines to the problem of unforeseeable and unfavorable developments. ITT Corporation asked me to review its start-up budget for a $400 million chemical plant. The budget forecast a cash break-even for the start-up year. I had one day to evaluate it, no chance to visit the factory site, and no background in the engineering or the industry. So I telephoned a retired chemical engineer with vast experience in starting up complex chemical plants (though none of this type). He told me, "Figure you'll lose about 15% of the plant investment, cash out, in the first year." I worked that number, backwards, into a detailed cash forecast that predicted a cash requirement of $60 million in the start-up year. The project manager laughed at me. The actual cash requirement was not zero, but $64 million.

The point of this story is not to show how clever I was or what a dummy the project manager was. The point is that a wise old man with a wealth of the right kind of experience could objectively dictate in 30 seconds the solution to a problem that the giant ITT had not been able to sort out, even with decades of experience and scores of professional experts in every relevant discipline. (We may assume that in the case at hand the ITT experts were not paid to be pessimistic.*)

It is also useful to note that the immense size of the project made the start-up loss easier to estimate. A tiny start-up operation, subject to only two or three variables, can go wildly out of whack. In a huge plant, with any luck, the problems will be non-cumulative and "swamped" by the total activity.

Do not be put off by the big sums of money in my illustration. Subtract a few decimal places, and you will have a situation comparable to your own new project. Do what I did. Ask around. Find someone who has done or tried to do the same kind of business, particularly an older person who can put his experience into perspec-

---

* I realize that my story contradicts my earlier instruction. I *did* just pick a number out of the air, 15% in this case. Nonetheless, it was a number well grounded in experience, and I had only one day to come up with it and prove it out. Further, it is a good story, and it is true, thanks to Dan Curll, the retired engineer.

tive. Do not reject out of hand the advice you will get from disillusioned and cynical informants. Listen carefully and ask a lot of questions. Their failures will tell you a great deal about what *not* to do.

If you are planning to open a small retail shop, walk down the street where you want to locate and ask each shopkeeper appropriate questions. If you are planning a new manufacturing facility, go to the local Chamber of Commerce. Then go to existing area manufacturers and ask about their labor relations, environmental problems, pending tax increases, and so on. If they do not want you to enter and compete for their skilled labor, they will emphasize the problems. Good.

After you have assembled all this information, recalculate your contingencies, show the total separately in your loan application, work out the consequences for your capital requirements (loan and equity). Now you are developing a good grasp of your new project.

Different Kinds of Things That Go Wrong

Here I am going to insert a subchapter on risks—different kinds of things that might go wrong. Perhaps it should have been a separate chapter. Yet I prefer to see it in the middle of how to prepare a successful loan application. Its position here emphasizes how critical risk assessment is to successful planning, a successful loan application, and a successful business.

Until now we have talked in general terms about being conservative in our forecasts, providing contingencies and margins for error. Now that we are getting more deeply into the principles and practice of planning, we must become more discriminating as to what kinds of things usually go wrong or might go wrong. And if things going wrong were not the norm, most businesses would not fail, so you had better pay attention.

There is no textbook or accounting convention that deals with this subject, and there is no standard terminology; there is, however, a world of practical experience. Let us bring it to bear on your business. We begin by sorting out conceptually the different things that go wrong and how they will affect your business planning.

Things that will certainly go wrong

The easiest category to deal with is the predictable: pilferage in a retail store, scrap product in a machine shop. These will be high until you learn how to minimize them; then they will settle down to rates that can be reduced only slowly. These "things going wrong" are provided for in your profit and loss statement, in percentages or absolute calculations. Only your experience and understanding of the business can tell you what size these provisions should be.

After you have reduced your pro forma profits by allowing for inventory evaporation or deficient product, you must turn to your pro forma balance sheets and make further adjustments for *future* losses—for example, for bad debts and obsolete inventories. In almost all businesses some bad debts are a statistical certainty, and some products on the shelf will never be sold, except as scrap or at distressed prices.

After you have done this you must go back to your prior period profit and loss statement and reduce your profits during that P&L period by the amount of the reserves you have established for future losses in the end-of-period balance sheet. If you do not understand the accounting, get someone who does to help you. Most businesspersons without some accounting background will need assistance at this stage, so do not be shy about asking for it. You do not have to understand the mechanics of the accounting. You *do* have to understand the concept and the purpose of the exercise: it is to show the real economics of how your business is expected to perform. In the future, when you prepare financial statements recording your actual results, these will have to show the same reserves, deductions, and write-offs, so this is no hypothetical exercise. These estimated costs and expenses will be as real as your payroll and telephone bill, and they cannot be ignored.

Things that will probably go wrong

This category includes things that are one step down in certainty from "things that will certainly go wrong." Although they are less predictable, they still must be taken into account. Here we are talking about major breakdowns of equipment, key employees who resign, strikes at supplier plants that disrupt deliveries, random lawsuits, burst pipes, and suchlike. There is no way you can predict such events, even though it is all but certain you will experience an unpleasant number of them. A practical and simple accommodation is to add 10% to your forecasts for the appropriate cost or expense category (e.g., plant maintenance, recruitment expense, cost of direct materials, legal expense, and so on). Or you can add 5% or 25%, depending on how you assess the risks. Include these provisions as separate, identifiable contingencies in your accounting work papers. There is no need here to adjust your balance sheet; the effect will pass through to the balance sheet from your pro forma P&L.

Things that might go wrong

The further down the scale of probability you go, not surprisingly, the more difficult it is to make a suitable provision. There is an extended strike at your plant; your principal supplier goes bankrupt, and you have no alternate source of key subassemblies; your major customer suddenly goes over to the competiton; a distant war increases the cost of your principal raw material 10 times. These are events you cannot foresee. If you had expected them, you would have arranged your affairs differently in the first place.

I see no logical way to provide for such reverses in forecast financial statements. Yet over a period of years one or a very few of them will likely occur. The solution is to leave them out of your forecasts but to provide a margin of safety in your financing resources. Your combined, untapped reserves and equity and debt capital should be sufficient to cover these setbacks. If your forecast maximum requirement for debt plus equity is $100,000 or $1 million, you might consider lining up contingent availabilities of $50,000 or $.5 million. This is an "order of magnitude," illustrative guess. It does, however, indicate how you should be thinking to cope with the need for unexpected infusions of hard cash.

Things that go completely wrong

An airplane falls on your plant, and you are not insured. To defend yourself against "things that go completely wrong" there is only insurance, and insurance will not cover ordinary business risks such as product obsolescence or changing consumer tastes. Take care that you are covered against insurable risks and include the premium cost of this insurance in your pro forma financial statements. The other risks, the business risks of starting a new enterprise, are yours. They are unavoidable, though they can be reduced by careful planning and their effects mitigated with an adequate reserve of capital for emergencies. The largest corporations in the world do it, even though they would seem to be the least in need of it, and so should you.

Union Carbide Corporation was a conservative, well-run company, as such dinosaurs go. In Bhopal, India, however, everything went completely wrong. Union Carbide's insurance will not cover all the claims against it, but the insurance will absorb much of the legal expenses and judgments. Union Carbide will probably be able to handle the uninsured excess by selling nonessential assets and drawing on its huge reserves of unused borrowing capacity.

So much for putting the various kinds of risks into perspective and creating a conceptual framework for dealing with them. Now let us analyze a concrete example: refer back to Chapter 2, and the footnote to the forecast profit and loss statements. This footnote showed the totals of the contingencies "things that will probably go wrong" that had already been included in the various line items of the schedule. These numbers were not global estimates; they were built up from realistic assessments of each type of economic activity (in $000):

	Period 1	Period 2	Period 3	Cumulative totals
Rework substandard product				
materials	—	2.4	7.2	9.6
labor	—	.6	1.8	2.4
Late delivery subassemblies (30 days)				
labor	—	2.1	6.3	8.4
interest	(2.4)	3.0	2.1	2.7
Engineering design changes	12.0	—	—	12.0
Raw material price changes (5%)	—	.9	2.7	3.6
Amortize additional tooling	—	6.0	18.0	24.0
Totals	9.6	15.0	38.1	62.7

(This example and the related financial schedules have been simplified to avoid accounting complications and to present the material as clearly as possible.) One obvious advantage of this kind of analysis is that it forces you to focus on concrete, individual potential problems; another is that it gives you totals that can be "eyeballed" to see whether they are about right for a business of this size and kind.

Now you are one step ahead of your lender. He was going to tell you all the things that could go wrong with your business. Instead, you will tell him. You have anticipated his objections, analyzed them, developed strategies to accommodate them, and shown them in your forecast. The loan officer is put in the position of having to criticize complex and carefully thought-out contingencies that *you* have calculated and substantiated. Imagine the interview if exactly the reverse were true!

A peculiar but surprisingly frequent problem should be mentioned here. It concerns a larger organization with layers of review that add contingencies at each level. Finally, the accumulation of contingencies, most of them unknown to the other parties, becomes so top-heavy that the project topples. The simple way to avoid this is to have each level add whatever contingency it wants. Just insist it is identified as such and explained. Then the highest level of review can eliminate duplications and assess the reasonableness of the remaining total.

This concludes our discussion of contingencies, and we will return to the main theme of this chapter, which is meeting the test of adequate earning power and cash flow.

For a new business, because it has no earnings record, the earning power test is the toughest. Many banks will lend to a firm with the most appalling economic prospects if it has had a satisfactory record of book profits, and they will reject the most promising new business simply for want of such a record. Do not waste time raging against this fact. Although banks are supposed to lend against future earnings, the basic resource for repayment of the loan, in fact they base their decisions largely on the past. If your business has no past, its future is considered particularly risky. This is true not only in the eyes of lenders; it is statistically true. Lenders' prejudices are soundly grounded in experience. Bankers are often shortsighted and rigid; they are seldom fools (except when they get caught up in the vogues that fool all of us every so often).

The most effective way to get around the objection of "no proven earning ability" is to buy an existing business instead of starting your own from scratch. Then, by adoption, you will have an earnings record. If you buy a money-losing business, you should have well-thought-out plans to turn it around and a record of sales on which to expand. As a rule, your banker will look more kindly on a plan to revitalize a down-at-the-heels enterprise than he will at a new business with no history at all (unless the old business has been taken over and failed anew several times).

My own inclination would be to find an existing business as a base. It can be had cheaply if it is run down. If the business is healthy, you are off to a running start. In either case you will likely avoid most of the costs of building an enterprise from the ground up, and these can amount to more than your intended capital contribution very quickly. (For example, the value of existing zoning and waste disposal permits alone may be worth the price asked by the seller.) These observations notwithstanding, there is seldom any point in buying a business in a declining neighborhood or a failing industry, however cheap the price. Only the shrewdest investor can succeed when major socioeconomic changes are against him.

Taking over an existing business and presenting a sound plan for improving it will overcome most of the bank's resistance to lending to a "new" enterprise. If you are starting a grass-roots project (that is, growing it from new seed), you cannot rely on a record of sales and earnings to support your loan application. You will need a much larger equity contribution to protect the lender's interests, and you will need a very convincing business plan. If you have a sound project and have read this book with understanding, you will have a convincing plan. Your loan application in this case will be almost coincidental with the project economics you worked out in Chapter 2. It will be well supported and persuasive, and it should largely compensate for the absence of a business history.

A valuable and often-neglected way to buttress your forecasts is with industry statistics. Most industrial sectors have a trade association which publishes composite surveys of members' financial results. These results are grouped by critical features, including member size and geographic location. Retail florists and hardware stores, machine tool manufacturers, suppliers of agricultural equipment, laundromat operators, major airlines, funeral homes, and—yes—banks all belong to trade associations which issue extremely informative surveys of their members' economic results.

These results are not confidential, though they are not public in the sense that you will find them in your local library. In your local library, however, you will find the reference books to get you started. *National Trade & Professional Associations of the United States*, published annually by Columbia Books, Inc., lists many thousands of trade groups. Supposing you want to found a foundry: you look up "foundries," and you will find a list of 14 organizations in this field. Then you look up each one in the main section and select those which appear most likely to fit your needs. Write to them to get the information you want.

In case your business is so specialized you do not find your trade group in that publication, you can turn to the *Encyclopedia of Associations*, a massive work in four large volumes published by Gale Research Company. In both publications many of the associations listed are only political pressure groups, societies devoted to arcane research or philanthropy, or other groups with purposes not relevant to your needs. You can weed out the nonstarters easily enough from the information given; the replies to your letters to the remainder will lead you to those of greatest value.

A larger bank might have these surveys. If you are alert, *you* will have them. Do not use them or refer to them in your loan application. When your loan officer comments that your forecasts are really only what you *hope* will happen, you say, "Not really. I have checked these forecasts against the regional results in my industry, and for a business of my size, my forecasts are very conservative. Let me show you the comparisons."

You know more about your business than the loan officer does. You have "completed" his general knowledge of sound banking with the facts of your particular industry and project. By putting these and other facts before your lender clearly and cogently, you are helping him to approve your application, which is what he wants to do, anyway. Indeed, he is paid to approve good loans, and if he does not approve enough of them, he will be fired. Hence you are to use your loan application and subsequent interviews so convincingly that finally the lender has only one question: *when do you want the money?*

Further support for your forecast earnings and cash flow can come from many sources. The local Chamber of Commerce (to which your bank may well belong) might have paid for a survey of regional economic growth and investment opportunities. Perhaps this survey is only provincial boosterism, in which case obviously you should not rely on it for your internal planning. On the other hand, your account officer might be unable or unwilling to rebut it. A municipal study of pedestrian traffic patterns might be available and might support your market survey. Extracts quoted from the U.S. Census of Manufacturers or your state governor's annual economic message may help prove that your business is in a rapidly growing economic sector.

Any such statistics or quotations should be targeted very specifically and should have a clear application to your business. Photocopies of articles with an immediate relation to your project—for example, a story about the recent stellar success of a similar business in a similar setting—should be attached to your application. The more concrete and applicable this background material, the more effective it will be. Research your industry's newsletters and journals for suitable stories. At the same time, do not give the impression that you are merely jumping on the latest economic bandwagon. When the popularity of hula hoops and bowling alleys reached its peak, that was the very time to avoid those businesses. A wise loan officer is leery of proposals whose main purpose is to latch on to the latest fad.

Business Ability and Integrity

As you have seen, there are many ways to increase credibility in your forecasts. A key one is complying with our third test: confidence in the business ability and integrity of the management and/or owners. For convenience, we will assume here that these two parties are the same. When they are not, your application should reflect that fact. Use your explanation of the relationship between management and ownership to improve your case. Imagine the best possible combination: a manager with a proven track record in this field and a wealthy investor who has successfully backed similar enterprises. Probably you are not so fortunate to enjoy that particular mix, but make the best with what you have, emphasizing previous management experience and accomplishments that bear directly on the new enterprise.

Like a good personal résumé, your description of management should be factual, not boastful, and oriented toward the job to be done. I would not attach old job-hunting résumés in lieu of a current description of your management: they were not prepared for this purpose, and they might suggest a failed effort to find employment. If previous experience was largely or entirely in a large corporation, emphasize specific responsibilities, authority, and independence. Even if you never managed a unit where you had full profit and loss responsibility, you may have run a department with a large staff and a sizable expense budget. Properly presented, this would show that you know 1) how to manage people, and 2) how to control expenses.

If your prior experience consists of failed enterprises, describe the enterprises, not the failures. There is nothing dishonest in omitting mention of a disastrous outcome. It is your experience as a manager you are describing. We all have Edsels in our past. (You will not see any mention of *that* debacle in a current annual report of the Ford Motor Company.) Discussion of past failures should be reserved for the interview where they can be dealt with in context (see Chapter 11, Revealing and Withholding Information).

Particularly if your management team is short of "hands on" experience directly applicable to your project, you should search your backgrounds for relevant accomplishments. Years ago, when I was looking for employment in international finance, a friend pointed out that my résumé omitted my command of Spanish! Maybe you are fluent in Spanish and your new retail business abuts a Hispanic neighborhood. If so, you may have an important advantage over a monolingual competitor. Explain that in your application. If you worked as a lowly storekeeper in the Navy, that is experience in inventory control. Community activities may be evidence of leadership and organizational ability. No one cares if you like to play bridge; but if you organized a major tournament, that might be relevant.

Perhaps no one in your proposed business has *any* experience in a key function. In this case do not ignore the vacuum; the lender will not ignore it. Confront it: we are now interviewing qualified candidates to fill the key position of sales manager; we have contracted with Price, Waterhouse to perform the entire accounting function; Dr. E. P. Wiseman, an internationally recognized expert in the field of materials engineering, has been retained to advise our firm on technical applications. The point here, as everywhere else in your application, is to demonstrate that you have thought out all aspects of your project and you know what is required to ensure its success. This will give the lender confidence in you as an entrepreneur and in your project as a sound investment.

Suggestions to Improve Your Presentation

Many investment prospectuses and loan proposals I have reviewed appeared to be full of pitfalls, shortcomings, and ill-considered strategies. Often, on questioning the promoter, I learned that he had already considered my every question and objection. He had an excellent answer to each one. He had worked long and hard on these problems and devised very effective solutions but had not described them in his application. He was amazed that anyone would be interested in that old stuff. Here the promoter was so engrossed in his specialized field that he failed to realize that the investor or lender is usually a generalist: the promoter should provide a layman's explanation of how the whole thing works.

Unusual technological or customer service requirements may require high levels of inventory; product warranties may necessitate large reserves for future repairs and maintenance; industry practice might dictate large discounts for early payment, resulting in a peculiarly low level of accounts receivable. All such "abnormal" conditions need to be explained in footnotes to the financial statements or in the text of the application. Chances are your loan officer will ask for an explanation of anything unusual, and your reply will satisfy him. It just looks more professional to have the questions answered before they are raised.

Also, there is always some chance that unexplained, peculiar numbers or movements in your financial statements will cause the loan officer or credit analyst such confusion and frustration that she rejects the application or becomes prejudiced against it. While loan officers do not have "production quotas," they do have work to get done. If your application generates more mystery than light, they may decide that processing it is a poor use of time. I have rejected proposals for no better reason.

Finally, a loan request over a certain amount or requiring an exception to bank credit policy will go to the bank's credit committee. You will not be invited to the review. You will not even be invited to stand outside in the hall in case someone has a question—and eight credit committee members can come up with a lot of questions. If the answers are not available from your loan officer or your application, action on your application will be deferred to the next meeting. Time, enthusiasm, and credibility have all been lost, unnecessarily. Your loan officer has been made to look incompetent, or at least unprepared. Your most important ally has been diminished.

By now, I hope, you will agree that all this comprehensive information in your application is A Good Thing. There can be too much of a good thing, however, and at some point your application can become too detailed, too long. The obvious rule of thumb is that the smaller the loan sought, the shorter the application.

Another reason for an abbreviated application might be an iron-clad guarantee from a third party (for example, your wealthy uncle) or collateral in the form of real estate. Such arrangements are a great convenience to both parties: you get your funds without a lot of hassle, and the lender accepts negligible risk.

I do not like them, for they evade the discipline which should be part of borrowing and lending money. Furthermore, the lender will charge you a higher rate of interest than it would have demanded on a direct loan to the guarantor, and you have ceded the advantages of preparing a thorough business plan and having an independent appraisal of it.

You may have been able to obtain the credit with no guarantee or collateral at all; you will not know if you did not try. Even if the lender adds a couple of percentage points to the interest rate to reflect the higher degree of risk, you still may be ahead. In the event that the project cannot sustain the higher rate of interest, it is a very doubtful piece of business to begin with, and introducing a guarantee or collateral to save it would almost certainly be unwise.

Let us return to the earlier question of the proper length of a loan application. Footnotes or accompanying explanations to "one-off" events and unusual figures should never be deleted for the sake of brevity. In case these are too long or too numerous to fit in or under a financial schedule, use a numbered reference ["(3)"] to a supplementary section called "Notes to the Financial Statements." A straightforward event can be set forth simply as a separate line item in the schedule: "Nonrecurring gain from sale of surplus property."

When all is said and done, the "correct" length of the application comes down to a matter of judgment. For reasons explained, I would tend to err on the side of too much information rather than too little. Backup material, as contrasted with the key financial statements, can be summarized in the main body of the application, and a complete story can be either referenced as available or attached as an appendix. Good candidates for such treatment would be a full-scale market survey or legal opinions on patent positions.

The text throughout should carefully eschew effusive prose ("incredible, mind-bending adhesiveness"), personal sentiments, or aspirations ("all of my life I have wanted to manufacture wooden aardvarks"), and unsubstantiated opinions ("I think this neighborhood desperately needs a shop to groom miniature French poodles"). If you think these made-up examples are too silly to be real, ask your local banker for his gems. Better, ask a dour, skeptical friend to read your draft text and delete all such statements.

When your final draft is ready, put it aside for a few days so that you can review it for the last time with a fresh mind (see Chapter 3). Ask persons who have not been part of its preparation to vet it for spelling and arithmetic. Ask a successful business friend to review it for consistency, completeness, and plausibility. If you do not know such a person, track one down through your friends. You are asking for only 30 minutes of someone's time, and few persons will begrudge you that. Indeed, most businesspersons will be flattered that you so respect their judgment.

During this final, independent review, ask your expert, "And what do you think of the project? Does it look like a good investment?" Since he has taken the time to examine the application, he will not mind giving you another 10 minutes to discuss the larger business context. Only a foolish person would embark on a new project without soliciting all the advice he can get.*

Big companies subject all their new investments not only to specialized staff reviews, legal, marketing, technical, and so on, but to final committee review by well-rounded, senior executives. These procedures are not followed because these firms have unlimited resources and nothing else to do. They are followed because they work. They help identify the bad projects and make the good ones better. Within your resources you must do the same.

At this time you should put your supporting documentation in order. Verify that you have the backup for each number, section, and schedule. It is extremely difficult to reconstruct and organize this material weeks after the application has been finished and submitted. Believe me, it is very embarrassing, when asked where a particular number came from, to have to admit, "I don't know."

Some loan applications include pictorial or graphic material, and I always like this when it is relevant—that is, when it helps me to better visualize the business as more than an aggregation of numbers. A business partly dependent on site location should include a map which emphasizes accessibility to transportation or customer traffic flow. A new consumer product should include samples of the product, its packaging, labels, advertising layouts, and sales brochures. In some cases a simplified engineering blueprint will help the reader grasp how the product works. Production, process flow, or store layout diagrams might be suitable.

The annual reports of publicly held corporations are good sources of ideas for graphic inclusions. Most larger libraries have a broad selection of such reports, and they will reveal a wide diversity of graphics. Avoid pictures of distant planets, unless they were taken with your new lens, or photographs of your firm's principals, unless they are demonstrating your product. As in all other aspects of the application, a key criterion is direct relevance. As in the text, puffery will be counterproductive.

Other firms' annual reports are also good sources as models for accounting layout and terminology. A related source is the prospectuses issued by businesses seeking to sell securities to the public. Many of the prospectuses are for relatively small and new enterprises,

* One easily accessible source of free advice is the Small Business Administration's SCORE program. See Appendix F, Sources of Governmental Assistance.

so this material may be more useful than the annual reports of large corporations. The prospectuses invariably include sections on Risk Factors, Management, Competition, and other areas you need to cover in your application. They are issued to raise money, which is what you want to do, so they make good models.

All retail stock brokerage offices have old ones lying about. Explain what you need to any salesman there, and he will be pleased to give you a fistful. Ask if he has one in your industry. If your project is a fast-food restaurant, the prospectus for a chain of such restaurants will be a gold mine of ideas.

Regarding delivery of your application, it makes a good impression to do this in person, to your loan officer. Make an appointment for a few minutes of her time. If she would like to scan it quickly then and there, fine, but this is a poor time to get deeply involved. You want her to have the time to read it carefully, to be suitably impressed by the excellence of your work. Ask when, roughly, you might expect to hear from her. Leave a phone number where she can reach you with questions. Assure her that you have detailed backup papers and that they are available to her.

8.

THE FINANCIAL SCHEDULES

Chapter 2 described how to set out the economics of your project. The new project, however, will not develop in financial isolation when it is part of an ongoing business. This chapter deals with using financial schedules to present both the new project and your existing enterprise to the lender.

In a sense these forecast financial statements are completely artificial. They are abstract representations of probabilities set forth in accounting classifications which are themselves abstractions, sometimes arbitrary ones. This is rather surreal, if you ponder it for a while. Yet this is the way the system works, and it is the best system for the purpose devised to date.

In another sense, they are not artificial at all. You will assign dollar values to economic transactions which you expect to happen in the future. The residual or net result of these transactions will be a change in your cash position, and *that* will be a very hard fact indeed, most likely the reason why you are in business in the first place.

Profit and Loss Statements

The schedule on pages 56–57 sets out a typical profit and loss statement (P&L) with both historical and forecast results. It shows the new project separately, as well as the incremental impact of the new project on the existing business. The figures for the new project are the same as those used in Chapter 2. Although this example is for a manufacturing/assembly company, the same format would apply to any enterprise. Only the accounting classifications or terminology would differ.

As in the Chapter 2 example, the forecast periods are not specified by year or any other time span. This is to remind you that the forecast accounting periods should be chosen not by the calendar, but rather to correspond with major changes in the progress of the new project, the progress of its cash requirements, and particularly the maximum cash requirement (Chapter 2)*. In the forecasts used here, these periods happen to be one year, which is convenient.

When your business is highly seasonal or there are other reasons for large fluctuations within the forecast period, then you have no choice but to divide the time periods more finely. The historical or actual statements can usually be shown by year, typically for the last three years. If historically your business experiences wide swings within the year, that fact should be pointed out:

> Sales of swimming pool filters to wholesalers are highly seasonal. A typical annual pattern of sales breaks down as follows:
>
> | *1st qrtr* | *2nd qrtr* | *3rd qrtr* | *4th qrtr* | *Full yr* |
> |---|---|---|---|---|
> | 65% | 25% | 2% | 8% | 100% |

Some such simple explanation is perhaps all the comment needed on previous years' annual results. In this example, however, there would be no way to escape full quarterly statements, at least, of *forecast* results.

In the following schedules all figures are in thousands of dollars.

---

*It is also wise to avoid specifying the expected calendar dates of events. For instance, use 1st Quarter, 1st Year, *not* Jan-Mar, 1987. The great majority of projects, for various reasons, experience delays in getting started. By using a movable reference point, you avoid the embarrassment of having missed a fixed target date as well as the need to explain why you missed it. If you waste six months in fruitless negotiations with your first candidate lender, when you apply to the second you will not need to revise your presentation to reflect the delay.

Of course this technique would be inappropriate when your project depends on a unique calendar event such as a centennial celebration. In this case you would do the opposite to show clearly that you realize time is of the essence.

As you can see, the format we adopted reveals a great deal of extremely interesting information. It shows, for instance, that you expect to have a sound, profitable business without the new project; that although the project is expected to lose money in Period 1, the loss can be absorbed easily by your existing business; and that during Period 3 the project should result in a 59% increase in total profits. This kind of scenario is a lender's delight.

Balance Sheets

All of the strictures about time periods given above and in Chapter 2 also apply to your selection of balance sheet dates. There is a device, however, that might save you extra work if your peak borrowing requirement falls within your standard accounting period. Let's assume that you are on a calendar accounting year—that is, you close your books as of December 31; however, because of seasonality your borrowing needs rise quickly thereafter, peak in mid-February, and then fall back to the typical, December 31 level by the end of March. In this case there may be no need to present twelve monthly balance sheets. Instead, you might include here a brief subschedule that describes the reasons for the mid-February peak and then sets out the resulting numbers:

> Because our major selling season arrives early in the year, the December 31 balance sheet does not disclose peak financing requirements. The peak requirement is analyzed in the table below (in $000):

	Jan. 1–31	Feb. 1–14	Feb. 15–28	Mar. 1–31
Bank debt beginning period	100	150	240	190
Increase in accounts receivable	20	120	(20)	(120)
Increase in inventories	60	—	(60)	—
Increase in accounts payable	(30)	(30)	30	30
Bank debt ending period	150	240	190	100

Although this summary table is not so informative as a full week-by-week balance sheet would be, it should give your lender the key information he needs. Indeed, simplifications such as this make your application easier to read and more, not less, intelligible. Just make sure that you have workpapers to support your summary explanation and that they tie into your full balance sheet. (For example, your

	PRIOR YEARS' ACTUAL		
	Profit & Loss Statements		
	3RD PRIOR YEAR	2ND PRIOR YEAR	1ST PRIOR YEAR
Sales (net of returns)	2,009	2,232	2,480
Cost of goods sold			
Direct labor	473	525	583
Direct materials	430	478	531
Depreciation	170	189	210
Factory overhead	320	356	396
Total cost of goods sold	1,393	1,548	1,720
Gross profit	616	684	760
Expenses			
Marketing & administration	284	315	350
Interest	32	36	40
Total expenses	316	351	390
Profit before tax	300	333	370
Income taxes	150	166	185
Profit after tax	150	167	185

	PERIOD 2 FORECAST		
	Profit & Loss Statements		
	EXCLUDING PROJECT	PROJECT ONLY	INCLUDING PROJECT
Sales (net of returns)	3,001	300	3,301
Cost of goods sold			
Direct labor	705	45	750
Direct materials	643	39	682
Depreciation	254	60	314
Factory overhead	479	42	521
Total cost of goods sold	2,081	186	2,267
Gross Profit	920	114	1,034
Expenses			
Marketing & administration	424	48	472
Interest	46	33	79
Total expenses	470	81	551
Profit before tax	450	33	483
Income taxes	225	16	241
Profit after tax	225	17	242

	PERIOD 1 FORECAST		
	Profit & Loss Statements		
	EXCLUDING PROJECT	PROJECT ONLY	INCLUDING PROJECT
Sales (net of returns)	2,728	—	2,728
Cost of goods sold			
Direct labor	641	—	641
Direct materials	584	—	584
Depreciation	231	—	231
Factory overhead	436	—	436
Total cost of goods sold	1,892	—	1,892
Gross profit	836	—	836
Expenses			
Marketing & administration	385	48	433
Interest	44	15	59
Total expenses	429	63	492
Profit before tax	407	(63)	344
Income taxes	204	(31)	173
Profit after tax	203	(32)	171

	PERIOD 3 FORECAST		
	Profit & Loss Statements		
	EXCLUDING PROJECT	PROJECT ONLY	INCLUDING PROJECT
Sales (net of returns)	3,301	900	4,201
Cost of goods sold			
Direct labor	776	135	911
Direct materials	707	117	824
Depreciation	280	180	460
Factory overhead	527	126	653
Total cost of goods sold	2,290	558	2,848
Gross Profit	1,011	342	1,353
Expenses			
Marketing & administration	466	48	514
Interest	48	—	48
Total expenses	514	48	562
Profit before tax	497	294	791
Income taxes	249	147	396
Profit after tax	248	147	395

January 1 Beginning Bank Debt of $100,000, as shown above, should equal the Bank Debt outstanding on the preceding December 31.)

I should point out that, in the example just given, focusing only on the three most important determinants of cash requirements is not so elegant as estimating every influence. On the other hand, since it is impossible to forecast correctly even the major flows of funds down to the last two-week period, in most cases further refinement contributes little or nothing to the real—as opposed to apparent—accuracy of final result. Specious or misleading accuracy should, in fact, be avoided: it gives a false impression of great knowledge and reliability, whereas in reality it is time consuming and meaningless. A knowledgeable lender will wonder whom you think you are fooling (maybe yourself!).*

Please do not apply this guidance out of context. If you are planning to manufacture ten million low-cost, low-margin wooden pencils, you had better have each element of your per unit direct labor and direct materials accurately costed to within $1/50$ of a cent. Well, whether $1/50$ of a cent or hundreds of thousands of dollars, I have solved the rounding problem in my financial statements by putting all the dollar amounts in thousands. This results in an automatic elimination of amounts too small to be meaningful, yet by showing figures to the last thousand dollars the schedules give the impression that the numbers were not just plucked from the air. Actual and forecast balance sheets appear on pages 60–61. Notice that they are laid out to conform with the profit and loss statements previously presented.

Although I used the same format for these balance sheets as I did for the P&L's, and the mechanics of addition are the same, life sometimes becomes more complicated when consolidating B/S's than P&L's. Hence I'm going to add some explanatory notes here, just as you would do.

Notes to the balance sheets (Pages 60–61)

1. The "working cash" requirement shown in the project-only balance sheets should not be required once the project is melded

---

*Years ago *The New York Times* reported an amusing incident of specious accuracy. U.S. senators on a committee overseeing Pentagon budget requests noticed that all the numbers were rounded off to the nearest million dollars. The senators concluded that this was proof of sloppy estimating and that the military procurement officers really didn't know what anything was going to cost. Thereafter the Pentagon assigned a budget officer whose sole function was to "unround" all the numbers in budget requests to make them look more accurate.

into the larger parent business. I have left them here only to avoid disturbing the numbers and making them more difficult to track. Similarly, I have left more than $400,000 in cash at the end of Period 3. In practice, most of this cash will be used to repay the owner's advances of $273,000, to reduce the "parent business" bank debt, and/or to fund new projects.

2. In Chapter 2 I explained why there would be no accounts receivable resulting from the project.

3. What was called "Work in Progress" in the project accounts is here included in "Inventories," of which it is a subaccount. When consolidating financial statements, as I have done here, it is often convenient to eliminate the details of the junior statements. These details remain available in a backup appendix or in file papers.

4. Most of the fixed assets in our existing business, including the tools and dies bought for the project, are used up within three to five years, and they have no salvage value. Rather than keeping this worthless equipment on my books, I've decided to scrap large amounts of it in Periods 1, 2, and 3 (excluding equipment for the project which, though fully depreciated, I left on the books for clarity's sake). All the gear scrapped had been fully depreciated. At the same time, I need to buy replacement equipment in order to continue my business. The table below

	Period 1	Period 2	Period 3
Fixed asset accounts			
Beginning period fixed assets	1,341	1,391	1,441
Fixed assets scrapped	(200)	(150)	(200)
Capital expenditures	250	200	230
Ending period fixed assets	1,391	1,441	1,471
Depreciation accounts			
Beginning period accumulated depreciation	629	660	764
Fully depreciated assets scrapped	(200)	(150)	(200)
Depreciation during period	231	254	280
Ending period accumulated depreciation	660	764	844

[Note that without this subschedule no analyst could understand the changes in the two accounts discussed.]

	PRIOR YEARS' Actual Balance Sheets		
	END OF 3RD PRIOR YEAR	END OF 2ND PRIOR YEAR	END OF 1ST PRIOR YEAR
Cash	10	11	12
Accounts receivable	342	380	422
Inventories	348	387	430
Total current assets	700	778	864
Fixed assets (d)	983	1,152	1,341
Accumulated depreciation (d)	(230)	(419)	(629)
Total assets	1,453	1,511	1,576
Bank notes payable (e)	324	360	403
Other accounts payable (g)	201	223	245
Total current liabilities	525	583	648
Paid-in capital	300	300	300
Retained earnings	628	628	628
Subordinated owner advance	—	—	—
Total equity (e)	928	928	928
Total liabilities & equity	1,453	1,511	1,576

	END OF PERIOD 2 Forecast Balance Sheets		
	EXCLUDING PROJECT	PROJECT ONLY	INCLUDING PROJECT
Cash	14	36(a)	50
Accounts receivable	511	—	511
Inventories	520	558	1,078
Total current assets	1,045	594	1,639
Fixed assets (d)	1,441	240	1,681
Accumulated depreciation (d)	(764)	(240)	(1,004)
Total assets	1,722	594	2,316
Bank notes payable (f)	454	336	790
Other accounts payable	296	—	296
Total current liabilities	750	336	1,086
Paid-in capital	300	—	300
Retained earnings	672	(15)	657
Subordinated owner advance	—	273	273
Total equity (f)	972	258	6,230
Total liabilities & equity	1,722	594	2,316

	END OF PERIOD 1 Forecast Balance Sheets		
	EXCLUDING PROJECT	PROJECT ONLY	INCLUDING PROJECT
Cash	13	15(a)	28
Accounts receivable	464	—(b)	464
Inventories	473	186(c)	659
Total current assets	950	201	1,151
Fixed assets (d)	1,391	240	1,631
Accumulated depreciation (d)	(660)	(60)	(720)
Total assets	1,681	381	2,062
Bank notes payable (e)	439	110	549
Other accounts payable (g)	270	30	300
Total current liabilities	709	140	849
Paid-in capital	300	—	300
Retained earnings	672	(32)	640
Subordinated owner advance	—	273	273
Total equity (e)	972	241	1,213
Total liabilities & equity	1,681	381	2,062

	END OF PERIOD 3 Forecast Balance Sheets		
	EXCLUDING PROJECT	PROJECT ONLY	INCLUDING PROJECT
Cash	15	405(a)	420(a)
Accounts receivable	562	—	562
Inventories	572	—	572
Total current assets	1,149	405	1,554
Fixed assets (d)	1,471	240	1,711
Accumulated depreciation (d)	(844)	(240)	(1,084)
Total assets	1,776	405	2,181
Bank notes payable (f)	478	—	478
Other accounts payable	326	—	326
Total current liabilities	804	—	804
Paid-in capital	300	—	300
Retained earnings	672	132	804
Subordinated owner advance	—	273	273(a)
Total equity (f)	972	405	1,377
Total liabilities & equity	1,776	405	2,181

summarizes what I plan to do and what I have included in my forecast financial statements (in $000). (See page 59)

5. My existing loan agreement requires that bank debt may not exceed 50% of my total equity. Hence in Period 1 I plan to leave some of my previous year's Profit after Tax in the existing business in order to accommodate this requirement. (Normally I declare and pay out dividends equal to my current profit after tax.)

6. At the end of Period 2 my total business, including the project, will be in violation of the loan covenant limiting bank debt to 50% of equity. But notice that my business excluding the project still conforms; only the new project causes me to go over the limit, and I have asked the bank for a temporary waiver of the 50% restriction to reflect the project's short-lived peak requirement.

7. *Note to reader:* The balance sheets show no accrued income tax liability; they assume such taxes are paid as the profits are earned. This simplification was made to help the less-experienced reader track more easily the key numbers from one financial statement to another. In practice you would, whenever possible, always postpone actual payment of taxes in order to enhance your cash position and minimize debt. A knowledgeable reader will find several such simplifications in the financial statements. They are intended to bring out the essentials of the enterprise as an organic, changing business. A complete and realistic chart of accounts would interfere with my purpose and confuse readers without an accounting background.

In writing such footnotes there is no harm in using the first person singular and in being informal; I've done it throughout this book. If your accountant prefers more conventional and rigid language, that's all right, too. Some loan officers enjoy the relief of seeing a real person behind all those numbers; some straitlaced types might be scandalized, though I do think this latter category is on the decline.

Funds Flow Statements

So far I have kept the accounting side of this exercise relatively simple. To continue doing so I will make a change in format now. Back in Chapter 2, Forecast Cash Flows were presented for the project. These forecasts showed all the cash flowing into and out of the project. This format is often called "cash receipts and disbursements." It is most useful for highly specific purposes and for relatively short time spans. It can also be used for your total business over periods of years, but it becomes cumbersome and difficult to manipulate for various accounting and practical reasons.

So, instead of forecasting the *total flows* of cash, in and out, in this section I have chosen to represent only the *net changes* in the accounts that affect the net cash balance. Here is one way to look at the difference between the two techniques. Suppose you had five different bank accounts and each month you added up the inflows and outflows of each account separately. Then you netted out the pluses and minuses of all the accounts and arrived at how much cash you had on hand. Alternatively, you could add up the *net change* in each account and arrive at the same net cash balance for all accounts combined. The latter is much easier conceptually and arithmetically.

Whichever technique you or your accountant prefers, there is a model in this book. An example of the gross cash flow method (or "cash receipts and disbursements") is shown for the project in Chapter 2, and the funds flow method is shown below. Forecasting all cash movements in and out certainly gives you a more detailed grasp of and a better handle on the day-to-day activities in your business, and many businesspersons use it to forecast and control cash movements over the next 30 days. Beyond one month, however, this technique becomes increasingly awkward, and its predictive and control values decline rapidly.

Please note that in addition to the forms discussed in this chapter, which must be included in your application, Appendix A presents a checklist of other financial subjects that might be included in your application.

	PRIOR YEARS' ACTUAL	
	Funds Flows Statements	
	2ND PRIOR YEAR	1ST PRIOR YEAR
Beginning cash balance	10	11
Sources of funds		
Subordinated owner advance	—	—
Profit after tax	167	185
Increased bank notes payable	36	43
Increased accounts payable	22	22
Depreciation expense	189	210
Total sources of funds	414	460
Uses of funds		
Increased accts receivable	38	42
Increased inventories	39	43
Capital expenditures	169	189
Dividends paid to owner	167	185
Total uses of funds	413	459
Net change in cash position	1	1
Ending cash balance	11	12

	PERIOD 2 FORECAST		
	Funds Flows Statements		
	EXCLUDING PROJECT	PROJECT ONLY	INCLUDING PROJECT
Beginning cash balance	13	15	28
Sources of funds			
Subordinated owner advance	—	—	—
Profit after tax	225	17	242
Increased bank notes payable	15	226	241
Increased accounts payable	26	(30)	(4)
Depreciation expense	254	180	434
Total sources of funds	520	313	913
Uses of funds			
Increased accts receivable	47	—	47
Increased inventories	47	372	419
Capital expenditures	200	—	200
Dividends paid to owner	225	—	225
Total uses of funds	519	372	891
Net change in cash position	1	21	22
Ending cash balance	14	36	50

	PERIOD 1 FORECAST		
	Funds Flows Statements		
	EXCLUDING PROJECT	PROJECT ONLY	INCLUDING PROJECT
Beginning cash balance	12	—	12
Sources of funds			
Subordinated owner advance	—	273	273
Profit after tax	203	(32)	171
Increased bank notes payable	36	110	146
Increased accounts payable	25	30	55
Depreciation expense	231	60	291
Total sources of funds	495	441	936
Uses of funds			
Increased accts receivable	42	—	42
Increased inventories	43	186	229
Capital expenditures	250	240	490
Dividends paid to owner	159	—	159
Total uses of funds	494	426	920
Net change in cash position	1	15	16
Ending cash balance	13	15	28

	PERIOD 3 FORECAST		
	Funds Flows Statements		
	EXCLUDING PROJECT	PROJECT ONLY	INCLUDING PROJECT
Beginning cash balance	14	36	50
Sources of funds			
Subordinated owner advance	—	—	—
Profit after tax	248	147	395
Increased bank notes payable	24	(336)	(312)
Increased accounts payable	30	—	30
Depreciation expense	280	—	280
Total sources of funds	582	(189)	393
Uses of funds			
Increased accts receivable	51	—	51
Increased inventories	52	(558)	(506)
Capital expenditures	230	—	230
Dividends paid to owner	248	—	248
Total uses of funds	581	(558)	23
Net change in cash position	1	369	370
Ending cash balance	15	405	420

9.

THE MULTIPURPOSE LOAN APPLICATION

The loan application described in the previous chapters may be vastly more comprehensive than would be suitable for a small loan, in which case you will have tailored your actual submission accordingly. However, the analysis, the thinking, the key areas of intensive review, and the financial schedules will be common to financings of any size. What you do not need to do for the lender in the case of a small or simple project, you still should do for yourself.

The Manifold Uses of the Application

If you have a small operation and a prodigious memory, perhaps you need put nothing on paper except the minimum the bank requires. If you are like most people, you will benefit from laying out your plans in the manner described and using that work for several purposes. Here are the uses to which you can put this work.

Feasibility study. The preparatory work done in Chapter 2 constituted a feasibility study—that is, an analysis of the economics of the project. This you would want to do even if no loan capital were required. Then, by combining the project with your existing business in Chapter 8, you determined that the whole makes sense. In short, both in isolation and in combination, the project is feasible.

Loan application. This use needs no explanation.

Investment proposal. If you wish to attract outside equity capital to your business, the work you have done will comprise almost everything necessary to present your enterprise as an equity investment opportunity. (See Chapter 19, Raising Equity and Venture Capital.) The only major points not covered would relate to the terms of the investment—e.g., class of common stock, dividend rights, percent ownership, and so on. These are often omitted from an equity prospectus anyway, since they are typically open to negotiation.

Obtaining supplier credit. The facts and picture that make your prospects creditworthy to a bank should do the same to a potential supplier. While a full-blown story should not be necessary for ordinary trade credits, parts of it might be valuable. If you are asking for a major concession from a supplier, then the entire presentation may be suitable. Your supplier's credit manager cannot propose an exception to company policy with anything less than a convincing story.

Operating budget. You also now have a reasonably detailed budget or business plan that you can use for internal planning, reporting, and control (except, as mentioned earlier, you may want to set higher standards for some internal goals, such as sales, than you set for yourself at the bank). You will probably want to go further than you did for the bank and break down your budget into smaller time periods, usually months, but that is simply carrying your existing work one step further.

Retrospective analysis. After your project is finished—that is, the originally planned time frame is completed—you can set down the actual results against the forecast. A comparison of the two will disclose where your planning went wrong, and this information is used to refine your forecasting in the future.

Much of the value of your earlier effort may be classified as "business planning," not strictly the subject of the book. On the other hand, if your watchdog can also catch mice, so much the better! It is just because the loan application has so many uses that it is worth more effort than an application in isolation might justify. It goes without saying that this extra effort will also produce a superior proposal to your bank.

Relationship of the Application to Your Business Plan

For those firms already strongly into business planning, it may be conceptually easier and mechanically simpler to turn the process around. Instead of the business plan resulting from your loan application, the application can be derived from your business plan. Sometimes I have used a company's business plan as the loan application, supplemented only by a brief cover letter. In most cases, however, this is inappropriate: they are similar tools, but one designed for the job will do it better.

Some banks do not like to see business plans submitted in lieu of applications. Business plans usually are—and in some ways they should be—overly ambitious, so actual results typically fall short of projections. After getting burned this way a few times, most loan officers look at business plans skeptically or with disbelief. The loan application, on the other hand, avoids optimism. It supports its projections by pointing out that, although the firm's business plan projects an annual sales increase of 20%, the application is based on more conservative assumptions. Describe them.

Finally, it is usually obvious that a business plan or prospectus to raise equity has been been prepared for another purpose. By submitting that document to the lender you are saying, in effect, that you want to avoid the nuisance of preparing an application. These remarks do not apply when the account officer is long accustomed to working with a client's budgets and business plans. There are other exceptions which the situation itself should make evident.

10.

NEGOTIATING TERMS AND CONDITIONS

In the phrase "terms and conditions" the two nouns are often used loosely and sometimes (wrongly) interchangeably. The word "terms" should apply to the rate of interest, the repayment period, and other facts which pertain only to the money lent. "Conditions" refers to accompanying restrictions which, from the bank's point of view, make the loan more secure or attractive in other ways. Examples of conditions (sometimes also called covenants) would be liens on working capital assets, restrictions on a second mortgage, an agreement not to permit net working capital or shareholder equity to fall below a certain minimum, a prohibition against other increases in debt or against alienation of assets, and so on.

Collateral Business

Another kind of condition is not included in the loan agreement—for example, the transfer of payroll accounts from another bank to the new lending institution. These latter conditions are not legally enforceable; they show your goodwill toward the new bank and generate a little extra profit for the bank in the new or expanded relationship. Confusingly, these extras are called "collateral business," in the sense of accompanying or related business, not in the sense of providing additional pledged security.

Collateral business is best kept out of the negotiations of terms and conditions. Your goal is to keep the pricing of the bank's loans and other services "unbundled"—that is, priced separately—so that each element of the package can be costed and evaluated independently of the others. Nowadays almost all banks do this internally in order to identify their most profitable services (so these can be promoted) and their unprofitable services (so these can be dropped or repriced). You cannot beat the bank at its own game, and if you accept "bundling" (this is the term actually used), you will probably be the loser. Without unbundled services you cannot check the prices charged against other suppliers. Comparing a bundled service from one bank to another is very difficult, particularly if the package is complex and you must factor in quality of service for several different products.

This is only the theory. In practice, you may be eager to transfer all your business to a bank in exchange for a desirable new credit, regardless of higher charges for collateral services (which may not amount to much, anyway). Do not offer to do so up front; retain this willingness as a bargaining counter to use later in the negotiations.

A discussion of collateral business came first because it is easiest, separable, and might help give you a feel for how banks think. "Terms and Conditions" are much tougher to generalize about, in part because they are usually interrelated. For instance, banks will concede a lower rate of interest (terms) if the level of security is markedly increased (conditions). Except when a borrower is so creditworthy that collateral and security are irrelevant to the safety of the loan, the terms will almost invariably interact with the conditions and vice versa. Even "triple A" borrowers have first mortgage bonds which take precedence over other debt and therefore carry a lower rate of interest.

Terminology

The word "terms" has been explained. The time period over which a loan is outstanding, the maximum life, is called "the term" or "the term of the loan." Loans with a maturity of less than one year are called "short-term loans"; maturities between one and five years are "medium-term loans"; and maturities over five years qualify as "long-term loans." With the exception of the short-term loan, which is always one year or less, and the medium-term loan, the final maturity of which is always more than one year, the terminology is not precise, though the indications given are generally applicable. To avoid confusion, find out what your account officer means when she uses these terms (that word again!), and simply adopt her usage.

Because financial markets and institutions are in such a state of flux, financial terminology is becoming less precise (or used less correctly). Avoid misunderstandings by agreeing on meaning. The moment you sense a possible confusion of meaning or intention, stop, and get it straight. (A few of my worst professional experiences resulted from a failure to do so.) Infrequently, self-important personnel will try to impress or circumvent you with unfamiliar terminology. Ask them what they mean. If you do not have the courage to ask them now, certainly you will not when it comes time to sign the loan agreement.

The Rate of Interest

Surprisingly to some, ordinarily this is not the most important subject for negotiation. There are several reasons why. The major reason is that for most new loans the interest rate is not easily negotiated down. Lending institutions are selling the use of money they have borrowed. They need a certain markup on their cost of funds to cover expenses, the risk of bad loans, and a profit. They make this calculation for their major categories of loans and arrive at the interest rate required for each category.* This becomes the bank's selling price for that "product," and the typical borrower can no more negotiate a lower price for that product than the typical shopper can negotiate a lower price for a standard product at the supermarket.

Here are the major exceptions to this rule:

1. A $1 million loan is, at the same rate of interest, vastly more profitable than a $50,000 loan. If the bank's pricing structure has not reflected this in your loan rate, you have solid ground to argue for a reduction. If your credit requirements are growing, you can ask for a lower rate each time your credit needs increase substantially. To qualify as substantial, the increase should be on the order of 100%, not 25%. Consolidating several sources of

---

*Consumer loans, for instance, are the riskiest and entail the highest cost to administer relative to the size of the loan. Hence they carry the highest rate of interest; look no further than the interest rate on your credit card balance to see the truth of this.

credit into one loan might also increase your average balance sufficiently to warrant a lower rate.

2. An exceptionally strong balance sheet or record of earnings is a sound reason to ask for a reduction in rate. Under these circumstances the bank can assign a lower-than-average risk to your loan, and the pricing should reflect this.

3. One or two years of a successful relationship with the bank, especially if combined with steadily improving operating results, is a reasonable basis for asking for a review of the interest rate. From the bank's point of view you are now a much better credit risk now than you were at the outset.

4. Assume another bank has offered you a better rate. Unless the new bank is trying to get your business with "predatory" pricing, your existing bank will probably match its competitor's rate. Such situations are discussed more fully in Chapter 14, When and Whether to Change Your Bank.

5. Ironclad guaranties or unusually strong and liquid collateral would clearly justify a lower rate.

6. In the case of a loan or a lease for more than one year at a fixed rate of interest, you are locked in, so a lower rate has relatively greater importance. If your creditworthiness later improves, you will not be able to use this favorable development to negotiate a better rate.

7. Changing market conditions or banking industry practice sometimes makes older pricing structures obsolete.

Such are the principal arguments for a lower rate. Here are some arguments that will *not* get you a better rate:

1. My business cannot afford to pay so much interest. [In that case your margin for survival is so small you are not creditworthy.]

2. I'm just getting started (a variation of 1. above). [That is why your rate is relatively high.]

3. I can get the money cheaper across the street (when you do not know for a fact that you can). [Then go across the street, the bank will answer.]

4. My business is certain to grow exponentially, and within two years you will have a major client. [Good, says the bank, when that happens we will be pleased to review our relationship.]

5. My firm will let all the bank's staff buy at wholesale directly from our warehouse. Or, more grossly, I will get you into The Best Golf and Country Club. [The first trade-off would not be acceptable in banking, and the second would be insulting. Only trade-offs within the banking relationship should be considered. For example, "In exchange for knocking one point off my interest rate I'm prepared to transfer to your bank my firm's large volume of business in foreign letters of credit."]

In connection with this last paragraph, I wish to digress to insert a short discussion on ethics in banking. While every year the business press will report spectacular cases of unethical or even criminal behavior on the part of bank officers or staff, these instances are statistically insignificant, even allowing for cases not publicized: there are about 15,500 banks in this country, with a total employment of 1.5 million. Financial institutions expect from you the same high standards of business ethics to which they adhere. If you cheat at cards, that is your affair. If you try to cheat your lender by, for example, grossly overstating the value of an asset, you will have acted very foolishly. Lightly given promises and exaggerated statements, perhaps ordinary and acceptable within your industry, are not accept-able in the banking industry. (There are always exceptions. In a few specialized industries chicanery is so widely practiced the banks expect it as a matter of course and are prepared to cope with it.)

This section on the rate of interest began with the statement that the interest rate is ordinarily not the most important subject for negotiation. The major reason was that in most loans it is not readily negotiable. The other reasons are:

1. If your loan officer concedes a reduced interest rate, he is openly reducing the bank's hoped-for profit; this makes him look bad. If he concedes a longer repayment period, he can argue that this will strengthen the loan and increase the bank's income; this makes him look good. Clearly it is to your advantage to seek the concessions that the account officer can most readily accept and advocate to his superiors. It is unwise to focus on the rate when easier and more attractive concessions may be available.

2. A point off the interest rate may not represent a lot of money for the typical small enterprise over the course of a year. On a $100,000 line of credit, with average usage of $50,000 and a marginal tax rate of 50%, one point would cost only $250. In relation to total sales we are talking of a tiny fraction of 1%. I do

not want to sniff at small savings as unimportant, but consider: a) Your time is worth money, and negotiations take time. b) Almost certainly you have bigger fish to fry. c) Almost certainly other loan terms and conditions are more important to the health and success of your business. d) Even if you do achieve a lower rate, the lender might try to recoup the shortfall elsewhere, perhaps in a way you cannot recognize. e) Most lines of credit are reviewed annually. If your business has done well, a year hence you can negotiate a lower rate from a position of strength. If it has not done well, at least the bank knows it is getting a premium rate of interest and thus will be more inclined to renew the credit.

3. A "rich" rate of interest is an effective way to get into a new bank. Once you are an established customer, the bank might make reductions to keep you that it would not have made to attract you in the first place, particularly if your business is profitable and growing.

Long-term loans at fixed rates of interest are another matter altogether. As you know from comparisons often published about residential mortgages, even a one percentile difference in the rate will create a huge cumulative change in the total outflow over 30 years. Finally, there are businesses that operate on such fine margins, typically in the financial sector, that one point in interest expense can mean success or death. Borrowers in these special situations are (or should be) aware of their circumstances, so there is no need to discuss them here.

Towards the end of Chapter 16, Keeping Abreast of the Market, there is a fuller discussion of variable vs. fixed-rate loans, the potential impact of rapid increases in rates, and devices to protect your firm against such increases. If you are worried that higher rates might seriously damage your prospects, review that chapter now.

Businesses diversifying into financing activities such as installment sales should look at the margins and dangers of the new project separately and *never* consider them simply as a logical extension of their existing activity. In these cases the prudent businessperson "lays off" the financing risks by contracting with an experienced third party, at least until he is confident that he understands the new business. Lenders' competitive bids and conditions, financial stability, and service reputation are vastly more important than when seeking a direct commercial loan. It is a different ball game and should be played as such.

Everything said about negotiating interest rates notwithstanding, you can still try to bargain for a better rate. Here's how. Leave it to last. Pretend to ignore the subject. Make the best deal on all the other terms and conditions, as discussed in the following pages. Only after they are settled, turn to the rate almost as an afterthought, and say, "Now there is one remaining point we haven't discussed . . ." Take it from there. Do not accept any linking of a rate reduction with earlier concessions on matters such as the repayment term. Other concessions were arrived at because they reflected (indeed, supported) the facts of your business. A lower rate of interest should reflect the soundness of the deal you have just put together.

In the final analysis, the key to the lowest possible rate is simply competition. As you negotiate with your several potential lenders, try to keep the resulting terms and conditions roughly in line, comparable. Then any rate differences will stand out as the principal remaining disparity. Try for a reduction from all the potential lenders, and then use the lowest quoted rate as a lever on the other bidders. Do not set up a Dutch auction atmosphere. In an ideal marketplace, this would get you the best price. In practice, most lenders will refuse to be drawn into that kind of bidding war. Your approach should be suggestive, not confrontational. Remember that at this stage the lenders still hold the high cards.

Calculating and Comparing Rates of Interest

This subject can become complex, and simple explanations may be misleading. This is discussed separately and at length in Appendix C.

The Term and Maturity Schedule

These are usually far more critical than the rate of interest. As explained, an extra point in interest is unlikely to affect your business seriously. A repayment schedule which you cannot meet, which leaves you insolvent, can be, and frequently is, the end of your business. Do understand that few banks will force you into liquidation if you have a temporary cash shortage (unless they are almost insolvent themselves and need the cash even more than you do). Instead, the lender will sit down with you to negotiate a "work-out" or "rescheduling." This will entail a higher rate of interest, more stringent loan conditions, probably more collateral external to the business (for instance, your home), and possibly interference with or supervision of the day-to-day operation of your firm.

You cannot eliminate this possibility entirely; you can shrink it drastically, however, by tying your repayment terms into your forecast cash flow. The project for which you borrowed the money will generate a cash surplus, and with this extra cash you pay down the loan in the amounts and on the dates agreed. Because of the margin of safety you incorporated into your forecasts, you will have sufficient cash to service the loan even if some things go wrong.

Since this model of loan repayment is so obvious and easy, why does it break down so often in practice? Usually for one or more of these reasons:

1. The forecast model is too optimistic, but probably not if you observed the ground rules laid out in previous chapters.

2. Unforeseeable and overwhelming macroeconomic events sweep your business into the trash can. The ten-fold increase in the price of oil is an example. By definition there is no practical way to protect yourself against such developments.

3. Microeconomic events such as changing fashions, fads, and technologies, plant closures, population movements, and new governmental policies can all bring large enterprises to their knees and doom small ones. In these environments the entrepreneur must sense the coming changes, make his money quickly, repay his loans quickly, and get out before the bubble bursts. (Difficult, but often accomplished by the shrewd investor.) Further guidance on this art appears at the end of Appendix C.

4. Everything goes wrong that can go wrong at the same time. This is unusually bad luck against which no amount of careful planning can prevail. After all, if you had assumed these conditions, you would never have gone into the business in the first place.

5. Bad management is the cause. In this case you are already in or almost in Chapter 11. (An excellent manual for firms facing insolvency or bankruptcy is the book *How To Save Your Business: winning ways to put any financially troubled business together again.* Arnold S. Goldstein, Enterprise Publications, Wilmington, Delaware.)

6. Your repayment terms are too strict. Here I can help.

My advice on negotiating repayment terms is very simple. If the bank will not accept a schedule that you know is well within your ability to meet, do not borrow the money. The bank, you, and I all know that you can fudge your forecasts to show that the cash will be available. If you do this the bank will probably recognize the forecast as "cooked." If it does not, and you fool the bank, chances are four to one you will lose the crap shoot anyway. And you *should* lose it. Your goal should be to run a successful business, not a crap game.

Although the standard bank loan requires repaying the principal amount of the loan in equal and regular installments, there is nothing sacred about this. It is merely convenient in the event your firm generates surplus cash in line with that schedule. If your business is highly seasonal, if you expect a plant shutdown for overhaul or annual vacations, or if other predictable events will create an irregular net cash flow, then the repayment schedule should reflect this.

You should request a "skip-payment" plan. Repayments can be suspended any time during the life of a loan when it makes sense to do so. In this context, look particularly hard at the first few months. Most loans are extended to finance income-producing activities, but few such activities generate an immediate net cash inflow.

So the critical question in any loan negotiation is: can I repay the loan when it falls due? Do not let the rate of interest, guarantees, asset ratios, or any other considerations distract you. You determined that you can repay the loan, back in Chapter 2. Now you must convince your account officer that you can, under the repayment terms requested, generate the cash surplus required. *Never* compromise to obtain a loan by agreeing to a shorter term than your numbers show is attainable with a good margin of safety.

There are several reasons why loan officers will tend to press for early, even premature, repayment. To avoid another digression, I will cite only one: they have been trained to believe that the sooner the bank can recover its money, the better. Do not argue with this artificially instilled wisdom. You will not succeed. Argue the economics, the cash flow, and the facts of your forecast. Because of your thorough preparation in this area, *you* hold the high ground.

Notes on Negotiating Tactics

As in any human encounter in which you are seeking advantage, do not press too far. Never say, "These are the logical conclusions of my calculations. Can you prove them wrong?" Say, "Our management team has spent weeks on this problem, and it's a difficult one. Let me explain how we arrived at our conclusion. Perhaps you could help us improve upon it." These two approaches will invite confrontation or an eagerness to assist. You might want to squelch an obstructionist by observing that his numbers do not add up. Instead, take him aside and mention he may have made a mistake; later suggest to him privately and casually some favorable aspect of your project he might not have noticed.

Sweet talk like this might be the wrong line when you get to the final conference. With negotiations between me and a giant bank at an impasse, my boss strode into the room and declared he was fed up. Other banks were prepared to lend to us on our terms, he announced. Then he left. In that case it worked because he was well prepared and shrewd.

In most situations, however, loan officers do not have enough at stake to be intimidated. Still, there are times to be aggressive, especially when you know you are right and sweet reason has cut no ice. Ensure that a more senior officer is present. Emphasize background material you suspect has been treated superficially by junior staff. At this point you may have little to lose and much to gain from confrontation: "Exactly what is wrong with my numbers (or management, market assessment, collateral)? What do you want to put it right? You're a financial man. Let's talk numbers." Never make any threats. The rejected borrower who says he will turn a bank's reputation into mud is talking foolishness, and the bank knows it.

Always remember the "what if" tactic to see whether you can gain an advantage more important than what you are prepared to concede. "What if I submit a monthly, instead of a semiannual, summary of orders received? Then you can cut back on the loan if I don't meet my forecasts." "What if I postpone opening the third branch until we agree that the first two are clearly successful?" "What if we make loan approval contingent on my major customer rejecting no more than 2% of my product between now and June 30? That will prove I can more than meet industry standards."

Loan Conditions: Collateral in the Business

Assuming you have not established your creditworthiness with a strong balance sheet or other credentials, the bank will ask that the assets in your business be pledged as security for your loan. This pledge might be a "boy scout's honor" oral promise not to remove assets while the bank is not looking. It might entail a segregated warehouse with an agent of the bank documenting each movement of goods in and out. It can be anything in between.

A related but different legal commitment is the "negative pledge." Under a negative pledge, the borrower agrees that he will not give any other creditor a prior claim on his assets or some specified class of his assets. Existing liens, typically a mortgage, are usually exempted, the prohibition applying only to future commitments. The negative pledge ensures that the bank's claim on your assets will not be subordinated to (rank lower in priority than) other creditors' claims. To put it another way, it forbids you to alienate assets from unencumbered ownership by your firm. Negative pledges can also encompass other kinds of commitments, but these need not concern us here.

The negative pledge is often the easiest to give, since in most cases it merely commits you to not take an action that you did not intend to take anyway. It is the simplest protection for the bank's position you can offer: it entails no record-keeping, ratio limitations, or reporting. It is also the easiest to modify in case a "one-off" event would require an exception—for instance, a special sales promotion or production run. Assuming the total credit relationship with the lender is satisfactory, you can ask the lender for a letter exempting your one-off event from the negative pledge. The letter would simply describe the exempted event, the value, and the duration.

An alternative and preferable solution in the circumstances just cited is to use the existence of the negative pledge to convince your supplier that a lien on his shipment is not possible or would require renegotiating your entire bank line. A negative pledge can, in fact, be a blessing when negotiating with other creditors: you just explain that this or that concession is prohibited under your loan agreement. Rare is the supplier who will tell you to go back and amend the terms of your loan.

A positive pledge of collateral, typically inventories and/or receivables, is more common than a negative pledge for a firm without a strong balance sheet and record of profits. It is so common and so commonly necessary that I advise against wasting a lot of time trying to escape this requirement. After all, it is far preferable to putting more cash into the business or giving a personal guarantee. Further, after your situation has improved sufficiently the lender may forgo this security.

There are too many kinds and degrees of collaterization of assets internal to the business to review them here. The rules of thumb, however, are as follows:

1. Resist pledging any more than necessary. This will maximize future flexibility.

2. Seek the least restrictive loan covenants you can obtain so that your business operations are not hampered or influenced by the loan's conditions.

3. Try to minimize reporting and paperwork requirements which create additional nuisance and expense. An obvious example would be a segregated inventory with receipts for each movement of goods and concurrent changes in the allowable loan balance. The best reports to submit are those you already produce for yourself.

Loan Conditions: Additional Equity

If the assets within the business are insufficient collateral to support the credit, the bank will ask you to inject additional equity or—what amounts to the same thing except for tax purposes—to extend a subordinated loan to the business. The account officer will say that without these new funds the business is undercapitalized. When a commitment to inject more capital is given as a condition for continuing negotiations, the lender is probably not bluffing. If two other candidate lenders tell you the same thing, almost certainly they are right.

Assuming that 1) you still want to go ahead with the project; 2) there is no other way to finance it (for instance, with advances from customers, extended credit from suppliers, or a sale and lease-back); and 3) you have or can raise the funds required, should you go ahead and do it? Let us suppose that the new project is a sure thing and that if the additional cash needed is eventually lost, it will not leave you and your family destitute. Under these circumstances the answer should be yes. If, as is more often the case, the situation is not so clear-cut, you will have to weigh up your overall position and come to a conclusion as best you can. This is a pure judgment decision.

How much equity is enough? Again, this is a question of judgment, although the lender's minimum may be your practical maximum. To the extent you have the flexibility, my advice is to err on the side of caution and to put in more than the minimum.

Some investors pride themselves on starting out on a shoestring, even though they have substantial personal resources. When they succeed, their accomplishments are reported admiringly in the business press. These cases make a good story. Very few make good business sense. If a business started on a shoestring can become a roaring success in four years, had it been properly capitalized it would have become a roaring success in half that time. Worse, the undercapitalized enterprise has no reserves of cash or staff, so any significant setback will quickly drive it to the wall. This latter outcome, while more common than the success story, does not make for inspirational journalism; hence it is seldom written up.

Many shoestring investors belong to the school "the more you give them the more they spend." This is a silly policy and a foolish statement. Expenditure levels should be determined by prudent management, proper budgets and controls, and careful assessments of opportunities. If your manager simply spends, like a governmental agency, whatever has been made available, then you are a poor judge of managers and should choose a different vehicle for investing your money.

Starving a business for capital diminishes its ability to survive, most obviously by endangering its solvency. There are less evident and often more harmful consequences. Management time is diverted from the task of creating a successful enterprise to endless credit negotiations with suppliers and other creditors; delivery of essential inventories is postponed to avoid cash outflow; discounts are not taken; the cheaper rather than the optimum choice becomes the standard; employee morale suffers; and the better staff leave.

None of the above is an argument against starting a business on a shoestring if you are willing to take the risk and have no choice; but do not expect the bank to make up any deficiency. It will not.

Loan Conditions: Outside Collateral and Guarantees

For reasons just explained, the firm should be capitalized properly in the first place. Collateral and guarantees external to the business operate to evade or defeat this condition. They tempt the lender to look outside the business for repayment, and this deprives the firm of the valuable discipline of being creditworthy in its own right. Finally, they usually result in an excessive debt burden; this in turn creates excessive interest expense, and the operating results are distorted and weakened by the attendant cash outflow.

Nevertheless, there are many reasons why owners sometimes

resort to external collateral and guarantees to make a bank loan possible. The worst reason, and a frequent one, is that it is easier to put up the guarantee than to put up the money. Investors who would not dream of selling their home to raise cash for their business will cheerfully use the house as collateral for a bank loan. If the need for cash is short-lived and the benefits "a sure thing," perhaps this makes sense. If the need is long-term and the outcome uncertain, the investor may be placing too much faith in the tooth fairy.

On the other hand, external guarantees and collateral are common and acceptable means of raising funds. Many entrepreneurs have no choice but to use them; they could never get under way without them. Each investor has to decide for himself. I know of no useful rules here other than the self-evident one: try your very best to avoid or at least to restrict such security, even if it entails onerous loan conditions and a higher rate of interest. Before you offer such security, make sure that any third party involved (a relative, for example) understands clearly the risks she is assuming.

An alternative might be to raise more equity capital from outside investors (this is covered in Chapter 19). The risk of losing your life's savings may be more serious than selling one-third of your firm to an outsider. Talk to older, experienced businesspersons about your plans and alternatives. (Your account officer should and will try to avoid counseling you on personal decisions such as these.)

A major supplier of machinery and equipment or inventory is a potential guarantor of a bank loan. He can guarantee your credit and take a lien on the assets he sells to you. If he has to make good on the guarantee, he can seize the assets and resell them, they are worth much more to him than the bank, since they are his normal stock in trade. The supplier can assume a higher risk on their value than the bank, *and* he has the incentive of his profit on the immediate sale to you. This is called "with recourse" financing and can be of great value. Do not embrace it without examining its costs and benefits, as discussed throughout this book.

Loan Conditions: Other Covenants

Depending on the size, complexity, and creditworthiness of the deal, the bank may ask for any of a great variety of special conditions to be included in the loan agreement. Most of them will be innocuous or at least acceptable. For example, the bank may want restrictions on payment of dividends or repayment of shareholders' advances. Generally these covenants would prevent only what you did not plan to do anyway, so do not turn them into points of confrontation. Do not expect that by arguing against and then conceding an obvious requirement, you will then have stored up a negotiating point to be used in another context. Borrowers who try this gain nothing; they sour the proceedings, lose stature, and waste time.

When a proposed covenant looks unnecessary or mysterious, always ask your loan officer what it means and why it is required. Often such provisions are boilerplate, inserted to cover all possible situations and not relevant to your loan. In this case, ask that the clause be deleted.

Keep a sharp eye out for provisions which are too strict or impractical. Examples of such provisions are:

1. A notice period of five business days, by mail, to advise you of an infraction of the loan contract or to convey some other important information. Fifty years ago, in a time of overnight mail delivery, five days was quite adequate. Today it is not.

2. A grace period of one week to "cure" a default. Loan agreements often provide for a period of grace during which you can rectify or cure a contravention of the contract without the loan being declared in default. Assume a couple of legal holidays, your absence on a business trip, and some misplaced messages, and the usual period is far too short for comfort. Your loan officer will assure you that his bank will not call your loan on such a technicality, and ordinarily it will not. Nonetheless, you should insist on a reasonable period to put things right. Fifteen business days should be your minimum.

3. Petty, technical violations which put the loan in default. These should be offensive to both lender and borrower. Insist that the word "material" precede events which might trigger a declaration of default. For instance, your loan agreement may preclude your leasing capital equipment. Would this also prevent your renting a Xerox copier? (Sometimes bank policy changes drastically. Loan officers may be told to liquidate all loans to a certain category of customer as quickly as possible. To conform with such a mandate, loan officers may call a loan on a technicality. Or a new loan officer may see your prospects less optimistically than his predecessor. These and similar arbitrary twists of fate are rare, but they do happen. Protect yourself.)

4. Provisions that are clearly inequitable. One gem I spotted was in a Canadian bank's deposit agreement (to be signed along with the loan agreement). It said, in purposefully convoluted prose, that if the bank made a mistake in its favor and you did not complain within 30 days, you forfeited any right to redress. If the mistake was in *your* favor, there was no time limit on the bank's right to correct it. No responsible bank would invoke such a provision to disadvantage a client, we trust, so why not insist that it be deleted?

5. Provisions that hinder your operational ability. In my eyes these can be the most objectionable restrictions of all, since they might force you into uneconomic decisions or to adopt expensive strategems to honor the commitment. Do not argue against such covenants with abstractions or general complaint. Select real examples to prove that your objections are valid: "Mr. Ciego, this requirement that I maintain a net working capital of at least $250,000 is fine for 11 months out of the year, but every March my inventories dip to a seasonal low (for such and such reasons), and this would put me in violation of that condition. Let's insert a 30-day suspension of the provision to accommodate this seasonal movement."

Compensating Balances

In this country, banks have traditionally derived substantial profit from a practice called the compensating deposit. In its simplest form it works like this. You borrow $100 from the bank at 12% interest; however, you are free to use only $85 of that sum. The remaining $15 is left on deposit with the bank as a form of compensation or payment. It is in your account, you borrowed it, and you pay interest on it the same as the $85 you are able to use. Clearly your actual rate of interest is not the nominal 12%. It is 12% divided by .85, or 14.1%. All the background to and consequences of this curious practice are too complicated to go into here. It should be noted, however, that the additional 2.1 percentiles in interest are not windfall income to the bank. This benefit is built into its pricing structure. When it lends without the compensating balance requirement, its rate will be closer to 14% than 12%.

In a variation of this practice, most banks will seek compensation through idle balances for other services rendered. You must maintain an average cash balance in your account sufficient to generate an implied or notional interest income to the bank. This notional income is used by the bank to pay itself for the services it has rendered you. The bank occasionally changes the notional rate of interest applied to your balance, and it also adjusts the calculation to reflect that portion of your deposit which must be left in its noninterest-bearing account at the Federal Reserve Bank. To confound matters further, different banks have different fee schedules, apply different notional rates of interest, and assume different subtractions for their Fed deposits. This outline is an oversimplification.

The way to escape these Byzantine complexities is to insist that you pay for services "on a fee basis," not "with balances." Insist that your interest rate be calculated on the amount available for use with no compensating deposits. Most banks are prepared to price their services and interest rates either way. In my experience, compensating with balances is almost always more expensive to the customer. The reasoning is as follows: When you maintain idle balances to compensate the bank, you do so with funds that ultimately you have borrowed from the bank. If these funds were not available to the bank from your balances, it would have to borrow them from the money markets. The bank can borrow these funds more cheaply than you can, by a wide margin. Therefore, in theory at least, compensation through balances has to be more expensive for you.

In practice, compensation through balances may not be more expensive if you keep substantial idle balances at the bank anyway. Ordinarily you would try to invest such balances short-term, but this may not be practical or worth the effort. Also, the bank will average your cash balances over the month and preferably over the year, so one very large deposit left undrawn for a few days may offset a small deficiency over an extended period.

Given the diversity of possible circumstances, there is no alternative to doing the arithmetic for each of your bank accounts at least once a year. Work from your bank statement, not your company cash book, to determine the average level of "free" cash you are leaving at the bank's disposal. Any textbook on cash management will show you how to do this and to translate the results into improved treasury practices. Cash management is a frequent subject of business seminars, so if your chief accountant is weak in this area of financial administration, have her attend one. There is no point in struggling to lower your interest rate by one point—and then giving up three points through poor cash control. This aspect of credit is reviewed more carefully in Chapters 17 and 18.

11.

LOAN NEGOTIATIONS

The loan or lease agreement and its associated documents individually and collectively constitute contracts in law. They can set forth whatever terms and conditions you and the lender agree upon, provided that:

1. each of you is legally empowered to commit your enterprise; and

2. nothing in the contracts is against the law or has been fraudulently arrived at.

The loan terms can specify repayment the first business day of the next year or the day after the New York Yankees win eight straight ball games. Nothing in law would disallow the latter payment term. So, within these very broad parameters, you and the lender can write into a loan agreement whatever suits your particular case. If your account officer seems inflexible and reluctant to depart from standard wording, keep pressing him gently but firmly for the deletion or addition of contract language you know would improve the agreement. The more precise and relevant the language, the better the agreement for both parties.

Loan officers and banks resist alterations to standard phraseology. Except for minor changes, the new wording will have to be reviewed by the bank's counsel. This is time consuming and, if the bank must go to outside counsel, expensive. Further, standard wording has been tested in the courts, and its meaning in law is well established. New wording introduces uncertainty.

So these are the pros and cons of "purpose-built" language. My suggestion is to prepare your own list of desirable modifications and then grade them as essential, desirable, or merely convenient. This will give you flexibility in negotiations and put the subject into perspective.

If you have never done it before, reading carefully every word of the loan agreement and its associated documents can be a grueling experience. I recommend that you do this and that you not sign without understanding everything in the contracts. You should grasp not only what the words mean, but what they are intended to accomplish and why they are necessary. If you are not familiar with this kind of quasilegal analysis and if the loan is large or complex, you should ask an attorney to go over the papers with you while you are sitting at his elbow. If your regular attorney has not worked extensively with loan documentation before, ask him to put you in touch with one who has. A lawyer experienced with the subject can do a better job of review in half the time. Whatever form your in-depth review of the documents takes, do not attempt it at the bank. Ask for copies you can take back to your office for unhurried examination.

Getting the Lender to Know Your Business

Assuming your enterprise is honest and promising, the more background your account officer has, the better. One obvious step is to invite him to visit your business premises. Bankers like to get out of their offices. They like to see where and how their loans will be used. An orderly and clean factory floor always makes a good impression. Show off your new accounting system; emphasize quality controls you have just introduced. On your home ground you have the best place for an effective marketing presentation. Invite your key staff to meet with the loan officer—not a perfunctory introduction, but a serious discussion during which your plant manager reveals his competence and understanding in detail of your new project. (By the way, there is no reason not to take key staff with you to the bank. You should, when they can contribute useful background and give a positive image of teamwork.)

Revealing and Withholding Information

In your loan application, do not volunteer unfavorable historical information such as a prior bankruptcy unless the application requires it. In the course of later discussions with your account officer, he will ask you about such events. Be candid. Avoid explanations that lay the responsibility exclusively on others, on factors beyond your control, and on unexpected developments. A businessperson who is completely a victim of circumstance, unable to determine or influence the course of events, is a poor credit risk. Instead, try to strike a credible balance: "A warehouse fire severely disrupted what had been a successful and rapidly growing business. Further, we did not increase our insured values in line with inflation. As a result we were unable to mobilize enough cash to resume operations. This certainly is the kind of mistake we won't make a second time."

Try to conclude any explanation of a historical loss or setback on an upbeat note. Not only did you correct the problem and learn from the experience, you actually benefitted from it: "We'll never get into that highly volatile market again." "As a result of that incident we put in new inventory controls to prevent it recurring. The new controls have reduced pilferage to almost zero and more importantly, they give us on-line data on stock levels for our twelve most important products."

It is unwise to conceal adverse past or prospective developments in your existing business. When the concealment is discovered, as it usually is, you will lose credibility. Try to leave them out of your loan application when they cannot be explained with a brief footnote (unless they are obvious and clearly demand a fuller treatment). Be sure to raise them during discussions when you can present the full background. Openness and candor will enhance your status; concealment will detract from it. Suppose you learn privately that your major competitor is about to introduce a new product or open a new store across the street. Say so. Explain what your plans are to react. Show what the "worst-case" consequences might be for you. All this instills confidence in your honesty and ability.

Exceptions to candor can be made, usually should be made, with personal matters and personalities. If your marriage is breaking up, that is none of the lender's concern. If you and your coinvestors hate each other's guts and disagree on everything, do not mention it. If your second-in-command has a drug problem, that is not relevant to your application. You are convinced your business will prosper and will not be affected materially by such problems, otherwise you would not be applying for a new loan. But the bank will not be convinced, for it will always shy away from problems that cannot be quantified.

If you live in a smaller community where a personal problem may have become public knowledge, it may be better to acknowledge it than to pretend it does not exist: "As you know, Mr. Hammer and I are engaged in an unpleasant lawsuit over a property we bought together some years ago in Nebraska. We have agreed, however, that this dispute should not interfere with our business here; and we have taken these steps to ensure that . . ."

I should mention that material and intentional concealment or misinformation about your business to obtain a bank loan constitutes fraud. It is a criminal offense. The bank's scope for exacting repayment and retribution is broad. Most banks will pursue repayment relentlessly in a fraud case. If the amount is small, most will not try to get you jailed because of the expense and unpleasant publicity. If the amount is large or if you are selected as an example, state or Federal law enforcement agencies will indict you, and you will probably wind up in prison.

Settling Terms and Final Review before Higher Approval

All credit institutions are structured to ensure that, except for very small loans, new credits or unusual terms and conditions must be approved by a higher or different level of authority. Make certain you and your loan officer have agreed on everything before your application is submitted for this second approval (usually by a credit committee). Do not leave any key points such as the rate of interest to be determined by the committee. Your negotiating leverage with that remote body will be negligible, and its decisions will be most difficult to overturn. Keep close track of what your loan officer is doing with your application and follow her pending submission to the credit committee.

If your account officer will permit, review her submission beforehand to ensure it is accurate and presents your case attractively and convincingly. If she will not let you see documents, insist that she verbally review with you the major points, her reservations, and her recommendations. Some account officers will resent this request and refuse. You should persist in reviewing the submission at least verbally. You have a right to know that what is being said about your firm is correct and the whole story. Your loan officer can and will present other views and information to the committee if she wishes, verbally and informally when your case comes up. This you cannot prevent. You can try to prevent uncontested and unfavorable information being included in her written submission.

12.

IF YOUR APPLICATION IS REJECTED

Assuming a lender thinks well of you and your business, he will not reject your application out of hand. He will explain that he would like to make the loan, but that would require additional equity, guarantees, or some other conditions. If you do not meet these conditions or negotiate a way around them, your application with that lender is dead. In this case, at your final discussion with the lender, be sure to ask the loan officer for 1) a clear statement of what would be required to be successful at his bank; and 2) his suggestions as to alternative means of financing your projects. Some borrowers are so disappointed at this point that they forget to ask these important questions.

Learning from the Rejection

A major reason to get a clear explanation of the rejection is that sometimes it resulted from a misunderstanding. Genuine misunderstandings sometimes occur between the most sophisticated borrowers and lenders. Between less experienced parties this happens often. "Oh," says the lender, "didn't you realize there would be a commitment fee? Why, that's standard practice!" Or, says the borrower, "Of course our margins have been deteriorating! That's because we are liquidating old inventories to make room for the new product. Didn't I explain that to you?"

Sometimes the "misunderstanding" is actually an error that crept into your presentation or into the lender's transcriptions and analyses of your data. A credit reference may have confused your firm with another firm with a similar name that had a bad credit record. The opportunities for error and misunderstanding are manifold. Make sure you are not a victim.

If your application was rejected out of hand, with perhaps no more than a form letter with a check mark next to the applicable, printed explanation, your prospects are abysmal. Nonetheless, you should call your contact at the bank and ask for an appointment. Explain that you do not wish to contest the rejection, you only want to have a clear idea of why it happened and what might be required to modify your proposal for reconsideration.

In the situations described above, unless there was a misunderstanding or error, you have negligible negotiating power. The best you can do is collect information. With this information you can return, sadder but wiser, to the drawing board. Can you reduce the scope of the project to require less capital? Can you raise more equity? Did you learn anything to indicate that the project is too risky or your experience in this field too shallow? You may be very discouraged, but you are not back to square one. Now you have vastly more information than when you started out.

Adopting a New Strategy

If you want to try again with the same lenders, do not return with a slightly modified proposal. This is time wasting. Your new proposal must represent a really new plan, one that has met the substance of the earlier objections. Without such substantive modifications, it is also of no use to apply to other, different lenders (unless you have specific information to believe they will be more receptive).

As in football: do not persist in a losing game plan. You are now well into the second half. A major change in strategy is your best hope, probably your only hope. Playing around with minor tactical variations is a loser's delusion.

Unlike a football coach, you have the option of simply walking out of the game. You can return to play another day when you have more capital, more experience, more status. Opportunities are seldom once in a lifetime. If you had the acumen to spot one investment with outstanding potential, almost certainly you will spot another later on, probably under conditions more to your advantage.

Appealing the Decision

Do not try to get to your loan officer's boss to ask for reconsideration of a rejection. If you are trying to get a refund in a department store, this might work; in a bank it will not. Rarely will a superior overturn the decision of his immediate subordinate when a loan applicant complains. An appeal that might succeed is "from the top down." A member of your board plays golf with a member of the bank's board, for example, and he suggests to his partner that . . . Under these circumstances you will probably get another review.

In a tightly knit community, where you can call on family and personal relationships, the right pressure may even obtain approval of your application. If the loan request was sound in the first place, good. No loan officer is infallible, and if you can circumvent a poor decision, I see no reason not to do so. On the other hand, if you misuse others to intervene on your behalf for the sake of a poor cause, you will be the loser. Generally speaking, getting a loan through favoritism is a poor business transaction. It may also be illegal, as many politicians have discovered over the years.

I realize some experts recommend appealing a credit turn-down. I don't. If your case is sound, the quicker and easier route is to apply to another lender, improving your proposal with the information you garnered from the earlier rejection. Credit equals confidence. If a lender formally rejects your application, he is not confident in your enterprise. This rejection, in itself, will create a negative atmosphere throughout the bank that will be almost impossible to dissipate. More specifically, an appeal means you are challenging the judgment of the bank's loan officer and credit committee. So the very parties you need most as your advocates become your adversaries, leaving you practically helpless in the ensuing struggle. Finally, many lenders will not even allow an appeal unless you provide such evidence as racial discrimination or violation of bank policy or procedures.

If for some reason (e.g., you are in a one-bank town), there is no alternative source of credit, accept the rejection. Wait a couple of months, revise your application to meet the earlier objections, and reapply with the request that a new loan officer process your new application.

Applying for SBA Assistance

One of the purposes of the Small Business Administration (SBA), a United States government agency, is to assist in the financing of smaller businesses which are unable to raise loan capital from private sources. The SBA works through the commercial banks. If your application has been rejected by two banks or more, you can request the least discouraging of them to forward your application to the regional SBA office. There is no need to list here these regional offices or to describe their forms and requirements. Your local commercial bank has this information or can obtain it easily.

When the SBA steps in and approves a loan, it will take part or most of the risk off the shoulders of the commercial bank by means of a guarantee. This guarantee can be for up to 90% of the loan principal, and it usually is (since by the time the loan request gets to the SBA, the bank typically has decided it wants as little of the risk as possible). Requirements of personal guarantees and the security of liens on your personal property are invariable.

All the banks and borrowers I know prefer to stay away from the SBA if they can, for several reasons. Firstly, and most importantly, when the loan cannot stand alone as a bankable proposition, without a government guarantee, then the project itself is almost certainly shaky. While 10% of a bad loan is better than 100% of a bad loan, it is still a loss; and the interest forgone and the administrative nuisance and expense to the bank may increase its loss on the transaction to several times its 10% exposure on the principal balance. Because of SBA restrictions, the bank cannot compensate itself for this extra risk with additional fees and an interest premium. Most banks feel, quite rightly in my opinion, that their judgment of credit risk is better than the SBA's; and they do not want to put their money on the line to be proven wrong.

Secondly, the SBA application is more comprehensive than that which the typical bank requires, and the processing of it will always be more time consuming. These comments are not meant to be critical of the SBA. As a lender of last resort it has to be more meticulous, and its insertion as a third party in the credit evaluation necessarily entails additional delay.

Thirdly, SBA participation will probably restrict your flexibility if you later need to move quickly to take advantage of new opportunities or avoid unforeseen problems. This is also true with your primary lender, but as a rule your local bank can react more flexibly on its own than in concert with the SBA.

These provisos notwithstanding, the purpose of the SBA is to help those who cannot get commercial credit without its assistance. If you need its help, seek it, and keep in mind there are drawbacks and strings attached, as described above.

There are other forms of SBA assistance to the candidate borrower (refer to Chapter 19 and Appendix F). The focus of this book, however, is the viable business loan in a competitive environment, and SBA aid is typically outside this frame of reference. Borrowers who do not qualify for a straight commercial loan can ask their local bank for further information about SBA programs; also, the SBA regional offices will meet with you personally or send you accurate and detailed brochures describing their programs. Do *not* engage an attorney or financial consultant to obtain information from the SBA or to apply for assistance from the SBA. As a rule, the SBA offices are well staffed to help applicants who are not sophisticated. You might need to hire legal or accounting experts for other purposes, but certainly not to deal with the SBA. Everything you require is contained in this book.

Countering Unfavorable Credit References

When the lender is relying wholly or in part on your personal creditworthiness he will check with a credit-reporting agency to learn whether you have an established record of prompt payment as an individual. The same check will be made on your existing business unless it is so well known and solid as to be above question. If there is derogatory information in your file, the lender may reject your application for that reason alone. If he does, he is obliged to tell you so. A few loan officers might not know the law and might be obscure on this point. Persevere with pointed questions until you are given exact copies of the offensive reports.

The principal credit reporting agency is TRW Corp. If you are covered by Dun & Bradstreet, an older agency which deals with established businesses, the lender will take your D&B rating into account but will be more likely to base its decision on its own assessment. The D&B rating is used primarily by suppliers to estimate quickly an acceptable level of trade credit, not by lenders to determine how much hard cash to advance.

TRW and all other credit reporting agencies are required by federal law to provide any applicant who has been denied credit a copy of its records without charge. You can get the name of the agency and its address from your account officer. If you want to see a copy of your credit record before applying for a loan, the fee is a modest $10. Anyone with doubts about his record of prompt and full payments should take this precautionary step.

Assuming your credit check was unfavorable, we can adopt strategies depending on the situation:

1. The information in the credit report is wrong, incomplete, or misleading. In this case you get the facts straight with the agency, usually by contacting the aggrieved creditor and insisting that he withdraw his unfavorable report. If he refuses to do so, send an explanation together with a copy of the correspondence with the creditor to your loan officer, with copies to the credit-reporting agency and the uncooperative creditor. [By the way, erroneous "facts" might be entered on your record simply because of human error by the many personnel who process the data and the absence of trained supervisors to exercise judgment. However lamentable this is, the other side of the coin is that these computerized systems provide convenient, economical credit to scores of millions of credit card users. Fortunately federal statute ensures that you have the right and mechanisms to challenge any errors.]

2. The information in the credit report is correct but can easily be amended to remove the adverse implications. For example, you moved to a new home and a legitimate bill was not forwarded by the post office. Erase such accidental blots from your copybook quickly with a copy of the settlement to the credit-reporting agency and the lender.

3. The information is correct but not applicable to your present situation. For example, it occurred during a period of temporary financial distress. A huge overdue medical bill subsequently paid in full is a clear example of delinquency which few lenders will hold against you once it is explained.

4. If the credit information is correct and unfavorable *and* you have no sound defense or explanation, you are, prima facie, a poor

credit risk. The best you can do is to pay off the overdue amount and promise the lender it won't happen again. Give a plausible explanation: I was waiting for an insurance settlement which took months longer than I expected.

Your candidate lender might receive unfavorable information from sources other than a credit-reporting agency—for example, your present bank or a trade creditor. In this case you also have the right to see the negative report, and you should react as you would in the case of TRW.

For the sake of completeness, I must add that I do know of instances of inequity (or worse) which resulted from personal animosity or venality on the part of banking staff or third-party informants. The point here is to waste no time in conspiracy theories or suspicion of slander. The real problem is almost certainly in one of the glitches already discussed. Unfortunately some loan applicants find it easier to blame "the System" or "Enemies" than to sort out the facts of their cases.

13.

BANKING RELATIONS AFTER LOAN APPROVAL

As emphasized in the Foreword to this book, your ultimate goal is not approval of your loan application; it is a successful credit relationship. This is an ongoing effort. If you buy a new car, leave it outdoors in the winter, do not maintain it, and drive it abusively, it will deteriorate rapidly and then break down. The same will happen to your credit relationship if you don't treat it properly.

Compliance with Loan Terms and Conditions

It makes no difference how warm your relations are with your loan officer or even the president of the bank. Your bank is not a friendly landlord to whom you can pay the rent a few days late with an apologetic wave and smile. The bank is closely regulated by federal and state agencies. It has to record your payment as late or your loan as not in compliance when this is in fact the case. The aggregate of such cases will influence your bank's credit rating, its cost of money, and its standing with the banking authorities. Never put a payment in the mail to arrive a day late if you can deliver it by hand and be on time.

When you realize that you cannot meet a payment or comply with any condition, call your account officer at once to warn him. With a minor problem that can be corrected immediately, a phone call and a simultaneous follow-up letter of explanation should suffice. Anything serious should be explained by you in person: why it arose, how it will be corrected, and what you are doing to avoid a repetition.

Please realize that I am not writing this because I am trying to protect the banks. I am writing it because it is your credit, your future, and your credibility that are at stake. We are not dealing with tenant rents or installment payments on personal purchases. Bank loans to businesses are a different ball game, and the bank makes the rules (to which, by the way, you have agreed in writing).

Reports and Information

Periodic reports required by your loan agreement obviously should be timely. Note briefly, without boasting, improvements over your forecast results. Explain unfavorable results and what you are doing about them. If you have had a serious setback, you should give this information to your loan officer in person and take a full story with you. Unless large amounts are involved, a verbal presentation is adequate. If over $100,000 is at stake or the explanation is complex, take with you a carefully prepared written explanation to leave behind.

Informal Communications

Every so often, use the occasion of your periodic reports to present them in person to your banker, even when there is nothing wrong. Tell him about the progress of the project for which the loan was made. Describe new plans, problems, and opportunities. This can be a general background chat or preparation of the ground for future changes or both. Possibly you expect to request a major new loan six months hence; now is a good time to mention you are working on preliminary studies. Your lender will always feel more comfortable later if he has had early warning of major developments.

The typical banker's psychology works like this. If you tell him six months ahead of time that you will probably be seeking additional credit and remind him three months later, when you actually present your request, he will be pleased. It will be a confirmation of your reliability and his expectations. Alternatively, if you just walk in and drop the request on his desk, without preparation, his reaction will be one of suspicion and resentment. (Same request, but lacking the groundwork!)

An invitation to visit your premises to show the results of a recent loan is always a good idea. If you like him personally, invite him to your home or club for lunch so he can escape the usual restaurant where he entertains customers. When your business is changing rapidly, quarterly or even monthly conferences may be warranted. When meeting with your account officer becomes a tedious chore and you learn nothing from it, reconsider the relationship. You are not getting your money's worth.

All the candor and bonhommie in the world may avail you little if your loan slides into default, but until it does, it makes for a pleasanter way of doing business. Besides, common sense says that an open and friendly relationship will be more productive than a cold and suspicious one, especially if difficulties arise. (Some "bankers" are so gregarious and friendly they give an impression of limitless generosity and accommodation. Spot them early and do not rely on them. These personalities are salesmen, not bankers. They have no say in credit decisions or in whether to help a client in trouble. They disappear at the first hint of hot water.)

Subsequent (Re)Negotiations

Most matters arising in renegotiations already have been covered under the subject of negotiations in Chapters 10 and 11. Here we will review only a few key points.

The annual review with the bank is the appropriate time to ask for a lower rate of interest and better loan conditions. If you do not have good reasons for the change, such as a much larger credit requirement, sharply improved operating results, or a much improved balance sheet, it is preferable to wait until you do. An exception would be if you accepted the original terms knowing they were too stiff but intended to correct them at the first opportunity. Another exception would be if you subsequently learned that you were paying "over the odds." Even if you cannot alter major terms and conditions, perhaps you can eliminate petty or vexatious requirements. Now that the bank knows and trusts you, it will more readily agree to deleting such covenants.

Your loan officer will probably agree to nothing material on the spot. She will "consider" your request. If, when she gets back to you, she offers any concessions, she will ask for something in return, typically more or all of your remaining banking business. Refer to Chapter 10, Collateral Business, and the next chapter on changing banks.

14.

WHEN AND WHETHER TO CHANGE YOUR BANK

The subject of this chapter is open to endless variations. It is almost on a par with "Should I get divorced?" or "Should I change my job?" As in these parallels, the answer generally is, yes, if you are unhappy with the relationship, if you have tried everything to turn it around, and nothing succeeded. The answer certainly is, no, if it would leave you on the street, destitute.

The Quality of the Existing Relationship

This should be the primary consideration. A bank that will stand by you during difficult times is worth paying a point more in interest, even more, assuming 1) the higher rate of interest does not have a serious impact on your net income; 2) there is a risk that some day your firm could be in trouble; and 3) then the bank will stand by you. The stickler here is point 3): you have no way of knowing.

In the larger banks the rapid turnover of loan officers is legend. In no bank is there any assurance that your account officer will not be replaced unexpectedly. Higher up the same problems pertain, and new uncertainties are added. Smaller banks are often taken over by larger banks, resulting in new management. Even a continuing management can decide to revise drastically its credit emphasis or lending criteria.

Very few banks nowadays function as an intregral part of a small community, knowing their customers intimately, and prepared, against their better business judgment, to help them over hard times. All banks want customer loyalty; loyalty to the customer is another matter. These statements are not made sarcastically or hostilely. They are the factual results of changing economic and social conditions. As a consumer of banking services, you want to know what the facts are now. A pious, idealized memory of small-town banking is about as useful as knowing how to shoe a horse.

Despite these remarks: if you have a successful credit relationship and a strong rapport with your loan officer, do not give it up lightly. Although its value may disappear with tomorrow's rotation of staff, more likely it will endure and serve you better than a new and strange connection. Even if we assume just a little loyalty and flexibility from your existing bank, certainly that is preferable to none from a new one.

Further, remember that while we are talking about banks, we are also talking about people. Assuming you took the advice in Chapter 13, Banking Relations After Loan Approval, not only will you have a good file with the bank, your account officer and her superior will be on your side when you need help.

Unsatisfactory Service

It is the responsibility of your account officer to ensure that the handling of your account is at least satisfactory. By handling of the account, I mean service generally, and particularly prompt and accurate transfers and bookkeeping. I have never met an account officer who could respond with more than sympathy to general complaints. Unfortunately, you have to log each delay, each error, each phone call not returned. Present him with the list. Without that tabulation of grief he can do nothing. Then add that you showed that list to Mr. Schreiber, the controller of Smart Corporation. Schreiber said that while his bank slipped up once in a while, he had no difficulties on *that* scale! Ask when you may expect to hear that these problems have been sorted out.

If the problems continue, you must present another list and be less agreeable about it. Accompanying that list should be a statement of the time your bookkeeper has wasted on these errors, the cost to your company of this wasted time, customer and supplier complaints you have received, and so on. Either this or the next time around, say that if the situation does not improve you will have to consider another bank. If you suspect your account officer is not doing all he could, say you want his superior to join you in a discussion of the matter. (Once you are an established customer of the bank, you can appeal all over the place and usually get some kind of hearing. When you were a mere loan applicant, that was not possible.)

Better Loan Terms or Conditions Elsewhere

This subject has been discussed earlier under other subjects. In the context of changing your bank, it is a straightforward matter. Your present lender has refused to concede the improved terms you consider appropriate; so you have gone to another lender and have been offered better terms. Would your present bank like to reconsider its position? I would always give my existing lender a chance to meet the competition, assuming he is otherwise satisfactory. I would never seriously consider a change if the advantages were minor. Of course, if you are not all that happy with your old bank, even a small advantage may tip the scales in favor of change.

A variation on this approach is to decide in favor of the new bank but ask the existing bank if it would like to participate in the new credit on the same terms. If the loan is large enough to accommodate two banks, the old bank will sometimes find this more attractive than meeting its competitor's price for the entire amount. This might give you the best of both worlds: a new bank, improved terms, and continuity with the old bank.

Before selecting that new lender, you should survey all the likely candidates and get quotes from at least two, preferably three. Again, try to canvass widely different kinds of financial institutions. Review Chapter 5, Selecting Target Lenders. Remember that you are not confined to a conventional credit from the traditional commercial banks. Unless your financial situation is shaky, these new contacts need take little time. Give them your historical financial statements, your forecasts, and your existing loan agreement. If they ask you to fill out a loan application, tell them you will do that when and if you apply for a loan. Right now all you want to know is whether they would consider offering materially better terms and conditions than you have now.

This very confident approach is suitable when the new credit will be essentially a replacement for the old one. If you have a new project to finance, a major increase in the amount, or a change in the purpose of the credit, you should be more of a salesman and provide more background. The early chapters on preparing a loan application will indicate how much.

Changing Your Account Officer, Not Your Bank

Sometimes you should not change your bank, you should change your account officer. An incompetent officer can work for an outstanding bank. Or perhaps there is a personality conflict between you and him which has nothing to do with his competence. In these circumstances it may be wiser to maintain a valuable alliance with the bank than to quit it because of one employee. Despite the personal unpleasantness involved, I would always prefer the former course. When you are a valued customer, the bank also would prefer this course.

Long ago you should have asked to meet your account officer's superior; that way, you will know her and can put your request before her. This should be done privately. Do not try to make a case against the subordinate. This will put her in the position of having to defend him (and herself as his supervisor). Describe the problem as "bad vibes," poor communication, misunderstanding, largely your fault.

The supervisor will not be fooled, and she will appreciate your tact. State simply that you wish to continue your relationship with the bank, but with a new account officer. The bank will oblige if you have been calm and nonaccusative. If you have been angry and vituperative, the bank probably will still oblige, though you will have given up some status in exchange for the identical result.

15.

USING SEVERAL BANKS

Instead of changing banks, consider adding a new bank. It may not be practical to split a very small credit line, but you could take on a new bank to handle only your payroll or daily cash deposits from an outlying branch office. Mention the change casually to your loan officer. Explain that you would rather have put the business through his bank, but Third National Bank seemed to have a very efficient and inexpensive service for handling payroll (or its branch was 300 feet closer to your branch office). The way you explain the change can imply a great deal without your actually saying it. To stimulate his competitive spirit, be somewhat evasive and mysterious. At the same time give a plausible explanation, e.g., 300 feet. From now on your account will have a priority of attention it did not have before. Your officer knows with a certainty that the new bank will be after you to transfer more of your business.

When you can add a new source of credit at the same time, that is even better. Not only can you compare terms and play one bank off against the other, you are no longer dependent on the credit policies of only one bank. Further, two banks will bring to your attention twice as many new products and prices as one bank.

If your business can support them and their prices are right, three lenders are better yet. Or four, and so on. At one point I was responsible as a corporate financial officer for 106 separate credit relationships. The whole credit machine had gotten out of hand. Try to find a balance suitable for your business. Each banking and credit relationship will entail advantages and costs, and these must be weighed. For example, a new bank might have a branch closer to your branch, but its transfer of funds to your disbursing account at your principal bank may entail an extra day of "float"—that is, nonavailability of funds to you.

Trade-offs such as these can be quantified with a bit of sharp arithmetic and close questioning of your banks. There are, however, nonquantifiable advantages to having several banks. They bring you more information, new ideas, and more competitive prices and services. A good new bank with a capable new account officer should offset an incremental treasury and bookkeeping cost of a few hundred dollars a year. If they do not after a year, try another bank or just return the business to your lead bank. As long as the new bank does not foul up your accounting, the cost of an experiment is usually small compared to the potential benefits.

16.

KEEPING ABREAST OF THE MARKET

Commercial credit has become an enormously complicated industry. For the average business, tracking and assessing what is available is not practical without a full-time treasurer. Even he would be considered ignorant in specific subjects, compared to the specialists in the giant corporations and financial institutions.

Take heart. An intelligent, part-time effort can pick up most of the available cream. The remainder, for most enterprises, would entail effort and expense out of proportion to the reward.

Key Money Rates

Every day *The Wall Street Journal* publishes a little box entitled "Money Rates." The first entry is "Prime Rate," and, to quote the *Journal*, it is "The base rate of corporate loans at large U.S. money center commercial banks." Most short-term domestic interest rates are, to use the trade expression, "priced off prime," 4 points over, 1 point under, ⅛ point off, whatever. The prime rate is generally a reliable and useful bench mark against which to measure your success in obtaining a competitive rate. Except when other rates are falling: then the prime tends to be "sticky" on the way down. Then banks begin to lend extensively at rates below prime to their best and largest customers, but they try to keep their *posted* or public prime rate intact as long as possible—for the rest of their clients.

You can guess when this is happening by following the differential or "spread" between prime and the "Money Rates" entry captioned "Certificates of Deposit" (CD's), which, the *Journal* explains, are "Typical rates paid by major banks on new issues of CD's, usually on amounts of $1 million or more." Your bank has many sources of funds at many different rates of interest, but even if it does not use CD's, the CD rate is a good indicator of its short-term money costs. If the 30-day CD rate is about 150 basis points (1.5 percentage points) below prime, then prime is about where it should be. If the spread widens to 300 basis points or more, as it did in August of 1982 and late in 1984, your bank's spread may be wide enough to warrant a reduction in the rate it charges you. Further, a widening spread usually is also a warning that the prime is getting out of line and will soon be falling. Your goal now is to negotiate a reduction in your rate earlier than the bank concedes it to all its clients.

When you attempt this, the bank will argue that CD's comprise only a part of its cost of funds. The bank must calculate its total, average cost of funds to arrive at a "blended rate," and this rate will include other, more expensive financings with longer terms consummated earlier in the interest rate cycle. This is incontrovertible, so you nod wisely and agree. Then you point out that if this principle determines its rate to you, why did the bank earlier *increase* its prime with such alacrity when its short-term money costs rose? The bank cannot have it both ways. It will find this argument very difficult to field.

You might not get your reduction. You *will* establish yourself as a customer to be treated with caution and respect. If the bank feels it cannot compromise its prime rate (after all, you might boast of your success to twelve other bank customers at your club), then the door is open for the bank to change the pricing on your loan. Instead of three percentage points over prime, you can pay two points over—leaving the bank's prime intact and you with an advantage of 100 basis points whether prime goes up or down.

Some banks traditionally defined their "prime" rate as the lowest rate charged their most creditworthy corporate customers. Then they lent below their prime to certain such well-regarded customers but did not extend the discount to other clients who, by terms of their loan contracts, were also entitled to borrow at prime, in the sense of the bank's lowest rate. A few of the latter group sued their banks to recover the difference. (We are talking here about large loans, and the 50 to 100 basis points involved added up to substantial sums over the years.) The banks involved got cold feet and settled out of court, presumably to avoid more bad publicity and because they figured a judgment would go against them.

This frightened many other banks into dropping the term "prime rate" and substituting the term "base rate," so your own bank may use the latter term. No matter. The prime rate is still reported in *The Wall Street Journal*, so you can easily compare it to your base rate, if that is your bank's terminology.

The country's most powerful and august commercial bank, Morgan Guaranty, was, to my knowledge, never threatened or sued on this point. It grandly and simply announced, "Prime is whatever we say it is." Hardly a posture to attract lawsuits.

Other Sources of Information

After published money rates, your next-best source of information is your business associates. Find out *specifically* what they are paying. Do not be bashful just because you are talking about money. If your colleague does not know, ask if your chief accountant can call his chief accountant to find out. In fact, your senior financial officer, even if he is only a bookkeeper, should belong to at least one professional association where he can trade information with other financial managers. Banking services and prices should be a regular topic.

Most of these associations are not nationwide organizations with high membership fees and glossy publications. They are informal groups of local financial, accounting, and treasury specialists who meet a few times a year to discuss common problems and opportunities in their areas of interest. Because these clubs are voluntary and informal they tend to be open and helpful; their goal is to trade information and ideas of immediate, practical value (such as which local bank is quietly cutting its rates to attract more business).

If you have a certified public accountant on your staff (or know one) she will be the best entry to such groups. Also, you can phone the treasurers or chief financial officers of any nearby large enterprises. They are often members of these area clubs, though you might have to call several to reach one who is aware of such a group. Don't be intimidated by big titles. If the officer is free, he will usually take your call after you explain your object to his secretary. You could also ask your local Chamber of Commerce for information. It is doubtful, however, that area lenders will be either knowledgeable or helpful in this connection.

If you cannot locate an association of financial/accounting specialists in your area, form one. The costs in time and money are minimal—each new interested party takes on the job of calling his share of other potential members, thereby spreading the effort of formation. Most established business associations, such as the Chamber of Commerce, are not suited to your needs. Their purposes are too various and diffuse, and their memberships usually include the local lenders who are, in a sense, your adversaries in this game. Your Chamber's directory of members, however, will be useful in identifying candidates for your group.

I should add that most small and medium-sized businesses do not borrow heavily or frequently enough to warrant joining or forming a professional club for that activity alone. The club should cover the entire scope of financial management, including such subjects as comparative evaluation of purchased services (e.g., local auditors and their fees), assessment of data-processing equipment performance, and the exchange of information on local overdue accounts payable. All businesspeople do this informally, of course; a common organization makes the process much more efficient.

Returning to published sources of information: very little of it is sufficiently detailed to be of practical value to the business borrower. *Fortune, Business Week,* and *Venture,* for instance, often contain fascinating articles on business finance, but they seldom get into the nitty-gritty of loan terms and conditions. They will report the rate of interest on a loan and then fail to specify the attendant conditions such as a compensating deposit or the transfer of collateral business. By now the reader will know that, without taking into account the entire package, the nominal rate of interest on a loan reveals very little. Indeed, it may even be misleading when quoted in isolation. (See Appendix C, Calculating and Comparing Rates of Interest.)

There are also specialized treasury newsletters oriented to banks and large corporations. These are expensive, filled with gossip about executive personnel changes in the big banks, and seldom report enough of the details of a new credit to give a reader the whole picture. In this last respect they represent only a small improvement over the general business press.

In short, I am not aware of any journal targeted at the business borrower; perhaps raising new debt is too much of a "one-off" event to warrant such specialization. However, periodicals oriented to small and medium-sized firms, such as *Venture, Inc.*, and *Entrepreneur* all have frequent coverage of debt financing subjects. And of course *The Wall Street Journal* covers everything, sooner or later.

Forecasting Interest Rates

In addition to wanting to know what the financial markets have to offer, most businesspersons wonder what they are going to do next or, more specifically, which way interest rates are going. Until 1978 the United States Federal Reserve Bank monetary policy was to control the volume of commercial credit by devices that, in effect, rationed the volume of credit. Interest rate movements under this old policy tended to be moderate, while the *availability* of credit tended to fluctuate wildly for the last 10–20% of credit the market wanted.

In 1978 the Fed shifted its principal control to "price rationing": it uses the cost of money, interest rates, to determine the supply of and demand for credit. While this change reduced one uncertainty, whether there would be any credit available for new loans, it introduced another for all nonfixed rate loans: what borrowed funds would cost "x" months or years down the road. For some debtors the difference between 10% interest and 20% interest can spell solid profits or serious losses. Further, since very high rates sharply increase the cost of holding assets such as raw materials, real estate, and common stock, the new policy drastically affects activity in every sector of the economy—thus the ceaseless preoccupation with the likely direction of interest rates.

Unfortunately, it is just like the stock market: no one knows. Some experts, such as the famous Henry Kaufman of Salomon Brothers, get it right for an extended period and then get it completely wrong. If you read the business and financial press widely, you will always find experts trotting forth seemingly excellent arguments—and coming to opposite conclusions.

Protections Against Rising Interest Rates

Instead of trying to second-guess the market, which you cannot do consistently, you should protect yourself if that makes sense for your particular business. For some firms the cost of money is too small a proportion of total costs to warrant protective measures; other firms limit dividends and/or growth to achieve this protection. Alternatively, you can seek term debt at a fixed rate of interest. Real estate mortgages and equipment leases are the two most obvious means of doing so. Also, some banks set aside a certain amount of their funds for term loans at fixed rates. These tend to be expensive rates, since the demand is so great for fixed-rate financing, but if it is sufficiently important to your business, you should pay the price.

Some of the more flexible banks offer minimum–maximum interest rates based on prime (also called "min/max" or "floor and ceiling" rates). For example, the bank agrees that regardless of how high prime goes, you will not have to pay more than 20% (the ceiling); and you agree that no matter how low prime goes, you will pay at least 12% (the floor). This creates benefits for both parties which might outweigh the potential disadvantages.

Another device is to arrange a mix of fixed-rate and variable-rate financing. Typically a mortgage on your real estate and a working capital loan based on prime accomplish just this. Some "what if" calculations based on different interest rates will indicate a prudent mixture for your firm. Although no one can correctly predict interest rates consistently, many businesspersons try; and some of them manage to get it right most of the time. They wait until long-term rates appear to be near a cyclical low; then they shift short-term and variable-rate debt into long-term, fixed-rate obligations. The immediate effect is usually higher interest expense, but if they have guessed correctly, in the longer term their total interest expense will be less *and* they will be better protected against very high rates.

A final device for protection is the sale of an "interest rate futures" or "financial futures" contract. This contract obligates you to sell (and the buyer to purchase), at a fixed price, $100,000 of U.S. Treasury bonds yielding a fixed rate of interest; the sale is for a specified date in the future, say six months or one year away. The theory is that if interest rates rise, your contract will rise in value. If you get it right, the gain in the value of your contract will exactly offset the increase in interest expense on your variable-rate debt. Conversely, if rates fall, the loss on your futures contract will offset the decrease in your interest expense. Hence, correctly done, the futures contract is not gambling or speculation. Quite the contrary: it "locks in" your future *net* financial expense, so you will neither gain nor suffer from interest rate changes, except for certain transaction costs described below. (By the way, you never actually deliver the underlying security. You sell the futures contract before it matures.)

This is a simplication, albeit an accurate one, of a complex subject. The major stock brokerage houses have specialists who can describe the contract in greater detail and recommend a contract with the terms best suited to your needs. Never use this device without understanding it completely, since it is not foolproof. Once in a rare while different markets move anomalously—that is, they get "out of sync"—and you could get stuck both coming and going. On the other hand, if your instrument is chosen correctly, the chances of this happening are very small. The administrative cost of the contract is not a major consideration: about $60 to enter into it and the same amount to close it out.

In addition, you will have to maintain with your broker a cash, noninterest-bearing deposit of about $3,000 per $100,000 contract sold. (If you sell several contracts you can deposit instead a U.S. Treasury obligation, the interest on which will be credited to your account.) If the market moves against you, you will have to replenish the deposit; if it moves in your favor, you can remove the surplus created. A typical one-year contract is sold at a premium of about 1% over current rates, so if there are no changes in rates, this protection will cost you 1% of the $100,000. Finally, if you wish to protect yourself for several years, you will have to "roll over" the one-year contracts as they mature.

As you can see, this is a complicated form of protection. On the other hand, it is typically less expensive than protecting yourself by entering into a fixed-rate loan. Any big stockbroker will have a free booklet describing these contracts more completely.

17.

FOR THE ADVANCED BORROWER

This chapter will describe strategies and concepts which go beyond the basics already covered. They are not really sophisticated, in the sense of state-of-the-art high finance, but they will require more initiative and imagination than most of the earlier material. Since you have been a careful reader thus far, you qualify as an Advanced Borrower, and you should read this chapter.

Overcoming Inertia in the Banking System

I have emphasized previously that all but a tiny fraction of staff in the lending industry are honest, and most are reasonably competent. Now I must admit that many, if not most of them, are unimaginative and/or timid. The average salesman at your local shoe store will show more initiative and a quicker grasp of your particular needs than the average lending officer at all but a handful of institutions. Why this is so is an interesting question; however, this is a practical book, not a treatise in sociology. This section will suggest tactics for dealing with the inertia of The System, which despite its ceaseless production and promotion of new financial products, still typically refuses to adapt its machine to deliver what the individual customer needs.

To illustrate this attitude, let me tell you a true story. In 1976 I was chatting with a senior officer of a major East Coast bank, and we got to talking about compensating balances. They seemed to me an unnecessary complication of the credit mechanism. No, he explained, they are an essential device to provide liquidity to the American banking system. Then why, I asked, do sophisticated banking systems do without this device in all other capitalist countries? The banker turned away frigidly to greet another client. This good man, with extensive foreign experience, was not trying to protect his bank's profits by dodging a sensible question. He merely could not cope with a challenge to The System which until then had formed his entire conception of banking in this country. Five hundred years ago the suggestion that the earth was round would have induced the same blank stare.

Shortly thereafter I set up a $25 million line of credit for Western Union with no compensating balances or idle cash balances. Usually bank credits (loans) are drawn down in installments, say $100,000 at a time, and the proceeds are deposited in the borrower's current account. This balance is in turn drawn down as the borrower writes checks against it. Banks like this arrangement because a good chunk of the money borrowed, even though the customer pays interest on it, is not withdrawn by the customer. It sits in the customer's account, and the bank can, in effect, lend it a *second* time.

The loan I arranged worked differently. Toward the end of each day, my chief cashier totted up his cash requirement or surplus, arranged a wire transfer to or from the bank for that amount, and simultaneously sent the bank a new promissory note for the new loan balance. Thus every day there was a new loan for the precise amount required, and the company's cash balance at the lending bank was always zero.

With this facility in place, Western Union no longer needed to fund the large day-to-day swings in its cash requirements by drawing on or adding to a $25 million portfolio of short-term, low-yielding investments. This expensive asset was liquidated. The simplicity of these changes was stunning. All it required was an account officer prepared to work out a custom deal to suit his client.

Some years before that, another company I worked for needed a sizable loan for working capital purposes but did not want any additional short-term debt to appear on its balance sheet. The banks were unwilling to lend medium-term. So we set up the loan to be payable 367 days after demand by the bank for repayment. The bank felt safe. It could see trouble ahead at least a year in advance; and the loan, in a sense rolled over every day, was always long-term (maturing or payable more than one year later).

These examples show how easy it can be to circumvent the conventions and prejudices of the credit markets. Especially, the reader will say, if you are treasurer of a large company. Well, yes and no. Surely I was privileged in the sense of being able to work full time at a specialized pursuit—and thus become more knowledgeable about my business. Also, lenders will be more flexible and spend more time on a large credit than a small one (which only makes sense). On the other hand, a $50,000 credit should loom just as large and important to a junior credit officer at a local branch as a $50 million credit to a senior lending officer at the bank's headquarters. The pyramidal structure of large lenders is set up precisely so that small borrowers can be accommodated by junior staff who are paid less and entail much smaller overhead expense.

In theory, the small creditor should be able to work out a custom loan with his account officer almost as easily as a large creditor does with his counterpart. It seldom works out this way in practice. The expense of a custom-made loan and the fear of the unknown and untested drive most lenders into long-accepted formulae and standard loan covenants. Although these conventions may not apply to your situation, or at least deserve modification, you can seldom find a loan officer willing to stick out his neck or ask his superior for an exception to bank policy.

To overcome this inertia, *you* must develop the special plan with its unique features that will make sense for your particular situation. Then you have to sell it to your lender. As pointed out in Chapter 5, the best way to do this is to have several potential lenders, preferably from different segments of the credit industry. Seldom will the Second National Bank of Prairie, Illinois, have a different mind-set than the First National Bank, which is just across the street.

The first obstacle you will meet when proposing an innovative package is that it is "against bank policy"; and perhaps your proposal *is* against bank policy, but bank policy at a very primitive and undiscriminating level. At a higher level, bank policy is always to make safe and profitable loans, especially to growing businesses. It is probably also bank policy to assist local entrepreneurs, create new jobs, and develop new financial products which can be sold to other clients. It is with appeal to these higher policies that you must promote an application for an unconventional credit. Obviously the higher policies will override the lower policies, once you can stimulate the interest of your account officer (that is, her desire for recognition and advancement).

If she is not responsive, ask her if you can submit the proposal to her boss. She cannot refuse. (Remember: in this scenario you are not trying to appeal a rejection of your application; it has not even been subject to formal bank review. You are trying to win agreement at some level in the bank that bank policy might be reconsidered in your case.) The boss might be more open or opportunistic or perceptive. Whatever the basis for your appeal, it should not be that you were treated unfairly or stupidly at the lower level. It must be that your proposal represents new opportunities to the bank that have not yet been exploited. Do not whine for money; describe new markets to your lender. Do not make exaggerated claims of new lending opportunities which the lender, with his superior knowledge of the market, might well deem absurd. Describe specific situations, comparable to yours, where your idea would be applicable and salable.

In both the examples of innovative procedures I cited earlier, my major selling point to the banks was that they would have a new product (that is, a new financing device) that could be sold to other borrowers. In addition to the obvious attraction of having a new product, the bank thought it could probably spread the one-off development expense (e.g., legal fees) over a number of new loans. This made the extra effort my loan entailed seem less onerous.

To return to bank policy: often the bank has no firm policy on the matter at hand. A few months ago I was hit with two $17 charges for overdrawn checks. That was bank policy. Five minutes with a junior account officer resulted in cancellation of the charges. Often a lender's staff will cite "bank policy" as an easy way to deal with a nuisance. It may be invoked by personnel on any level of authority to avoid thinking out a problem not covered in the manual. Sometimes staff pick up misinformation from colleagues and, not knowing any better, incorporate it into their knowledge of "policy."

After "bank policy" the next line of rejection is, "It's against the law." Or against Comptroller of Currency Regulations. This response is frequently as spurious and ill informed as the Bank Policy Defense. Only a tiny few of a lending firm's employees have specific and accurate knowledge of the complex and numerous laws and regulations that govern commercial credit. Your first response should be: show me a copy of the law or regulation. In my experience, it will never be produced for your inspection.

Assuming the rare case that the lender produces a legal prohibition, your second response is: how do we get around it? No governmental entity has yet devised a commercial law that cannot be circumvented. If the economics of your project are sound, you must try to devise a way around the law.

I do not advocate breaking the law. But I do insist that there are stupid and poorly framed laws, especially in banking, and these usually can be circumvented. If the largest U.S. bank, Citibank, can do this as a matter of policy and routinely, I see nothing wrong in we lesser enterprises doing likewise. As a rule, it is your persistence and imagination which must provide the engine. Unless you are lucky, your lender will not provide the impetus. By persisting and reaching a higher officer, you will probably get your new scheme an intelligent hearing. If your idea makes sense, at this point your skeptical adversary, your lender, might well become your enthusiastic champion!

Taking Advantage of Promotions

For the borrower who can afford to pick and choose, the best lender of all is the lender who is hungry for new business. This lender sends cohorts of young representatives out into the field to sell money at below-market rates or under unusually favorable conditions. They are a godsend to the sophisticated borrower. They are partly on commission or bonus and do not care a tittle whether the loans they arrange will ever be repaid. Seize these boys with both hands.

They represent the worst of the lending industry—and your golden opportunity to borrow advantageously. They are pumped-up salesmen with quotas to meet and huge year-end rewards to look forward to. I love them.

There are catches. Clearly the lending institution employing these clowns will soon be in trouble. So your loan documentation must be complete and careful. You must comply religiously with all loan conditions. Then the lender will have no basis for canceling the credits he belatedly realizes were foolish and unprofitable. In the most extreme cases, when the lender's portfolio has too high a mixture of uncollectable and unprofitable loans, he will go El Foldo. If he is not rescued and actually goes into bankruptcy, your loan might be called, since the bankruptcy court has the power to nullify any and all contracts, including yours. These cases are very rare, however—too rare to warrant forgoing an obvious windfall.

[Do beware the counter-entry to these transactions: deposits. Institutions offering interest rates on deposits that are significantly higher than the market, unless they are short-lived promotions, are almost always in trouble. Never lend them your money on deposit, regardless of their claims of Federal and state insurance backing, without the most careful investigation.]

Sometimes lenders offering "free lunches" are really conducting well-considered promotions, not unlike a supermarket 1¢ sale. These are loss-leaders, intended to bring in new business. Clearly you are not going to move your banking business for a penny can of powdered orange juice. You should be receptive to the message: the lender wants more business and is willing to discount his goods, temporarily, to obtain it. It is up to you as a shrewd businessperson to convert that temporary discount into a permanent advantage. If you are able to accomplish this through a well-emplaced account officer who will take a continuing responsibility for your account, fine. Otherwise, forget it. The game is not worth the candle. To a busy manager, one who has many other fish to fry, the time and nuisance costs of a new credit arrangement invariably exceed a temporary saving in interest expense.

Cash and Debt: The Concept of Fungibility

Cash and debt, or credit, are fungible; that is, they are interchangeable. If this is not self-evident, consider a $25 purchase at a local shop. You can pay for it with the banknotes in your pocket or the credit card in your wallet. For a business the principle is the same, though in practice the mechanics are different. You can use the day's cash receipts to increase your cash balance at the bank (in anticipation of tomorrow's cash disbursements) or to decrease your loan outstanding (assuming you have that flexibility). When you need to pay a supplier, you can write a check against your cash balance if it is sufficient; if it is insufficient, you can draw down your line of credit, thereby increasing your available cash. The supplier is indifferent as to the source of his payment, as long as its color is green.

Indifferent to the payee, the source of payment is not a matter of indifference to the payor. Payments from a source of credit cost money (interest), whereas payments from idle cash cost him nothing (or, if he maintains his idle cash in short-term investments, the cost to him of interest income forgone is less than the cost of increasing his borrowing). These truisms are as obvious as those in the paragraph above. Nonetheless, most small companies (and individuals) ignore them, and thereby they enrich their lenders unnecessarily.

This was demonstrated in a study conducted by the Caruth Institute of Owner-Managed Business at Southern Methodist University. The study, based on a major bank's own cost accounting system, showed that the bank's pre-tax earnings on small business loans were 2.7 percentage points higher than its earnings on loans to large firms, despite the greater risk and the higher administrative expense of the small loans. Not 2.7% higher, mind you, but 270 basis points higher! This is equivalent to paying 17.7% interest instead of 15.0% interest.

Why was this so? Because the smaller firms, relative to their size, left more of their funds in idle cash deposits than the large firms. In other words, the small businessman is not acting on the fungibility and relative cost of his two sources of funds, cash and credit. To put it more graphically, these borrowers, who probably fought tooth and nail for a one-half percentage point reduction in their interest rate, turn around and give back to the lender *five times* that amount in the value of the idle cash that belongs to them.

The bank takes the depositor's idle balance and lends it elsewhere at no cost of funds to the bank. The profit on this is comparable to what a secretarial services agency would earn if it did not pay anything for its secretaries. Devices for transferring this bonus from the bank back into your own pocket are described in the following chapter, Cash Management and the Cost of Credit.

18.

CASH MANAGEMENT AND THE COST OF CREDIT

From the preceding chapter it should be apparent that the major *controllable* factor in your total cost of credit/cash/money is how well you manage your cash. The stated interest rate on your loan is an obvious, hard, and painful number. The cost of idle funds is invisible and insidious. Even when the borrower recognizes it, he will typically explain it away: it's a kind of "slop fund" to accommodate the irregularities of receipts and disbursements; it looks good on the balance sheet; the bank likes it; it's an emergency reserve. Each of these rationalizations may have some validity. Each purpose, however, can be achieved less expensively than by maintaining excessive cash balances.

Purpose: To Accommodate Swings in Cash Flow

Solution A. The optimum solution is what is called a "zero balance account." This arrangement means that at the end of each day your bank's computer nets all the transactions that have hit your account that day—both debits and credits—and it automatically increases or decreases your credit outstanding to arrive at a zero balance in your cash account. The amount of your line of credit is large enough to accommodate any reasonably foreseeable excess of disbursements over receipts. At the same time you are deeply enough into the line of credit to ensure that a reverse excess—an idle cash balance—will not occur.

To illustrate: you study your historical swings in minimum/maximum cash requirements; then you adjust these extremes, if that is indicated, by your financial plan for the next twelve months. Suppose the min/max swing is $50,000. You set up a zero balance account in conjunction with an overdraft-type credit facility for $100,000. Assuming you are just now in the middle of your expected swing-range, you immediately draw down $40,000 to use in your business on a continuing basis. Now we can show what you have arranged in tabular form:

	Typical debt	Maximum debt	Minimum debt
Overdraft outstanding	$ 40,000	$ 65,000	$ 15,000
Unused overdraft	60,000	35,000	85,000
Total credit line	$100,000	$100,000	$100,000

You will note that in this example the targeted typical or average debt level is pitched at $40,000 rather than $50,000 (which would be the exact middle of your total line of credit). The reason is that in financing your business you should always err on the side of caution. If you experience a temporary cash surplus due to unforeseen events, the cost to you is small; if your requirements exceed your limit, the consequences could be disastrous.

The little model presented above is basically what Merrill Lynch offers retail customers with its hugely successful Cash Management Account. (Minus the feature of investing and paying interest on any net cash position; but that, too, can be incorporated into an overdraft-type bank credit if the sums involved are large enough.) Your local bank officer may tell you that it cannot be done, meaning that the bank has not done it yet and/or existing arrangements are too lucrative to consider changing. But I tell you it *can* be done. I have done it (see Chapter 17); hundreds of corporations do it; and more than one million customers of Merrill Lynch do it. All that is required is a willing bank and conformity with certain archaic banking regulations.

By the time you read this, even the second requirement may have disappeared.

This is not a free lunch for either you or the bank. The bank gives up no-cost idle deposits and might incur additional expense. You will pay a higher nominal rate of interest to compensate the bank for these disadvantages. However, if you strike the right balance, both will benefit. You will gain a lower total interest expense (including the cost to you of idle balances), and the bank will gain a new account (or avoid losing an existing account to another bank).

Solution B. Suppose you are stuck with idle balances. You are not able to arrange a zero-balance line of credit; you must borrow in "lumps" of credit that meet your cash requirements only very roughly and leave you with sporadic wads of cash you cannot employ. In this case you and your account officer place a value on your idle cash (see Chapter 10, Compensating Balances).

This approach is 1) less economical than a zero-balance account, but 2) less expensive than ignoring your idle balances, assuming they average more than a few hundred dollars (in which case they are not worth valuing). Negotiating an imputed interest rate on idle balances is usually difficult when the amounts are not significant. The bank will have a standard rate, and it is unlikely you can effect a higher one. The difference between the bank's standard rate and what you might negotiate is probably too small to quarrel about. This observation can be expanded into a generalization: usually you can achieve a major improvement in your total cost of credit only from a new type of borrowing arrangement; winning an adjustment upwards of the bank's formula for calculating imputed interest, for example, will seldom yield more than a few extra dollars a month.

The banks' formulae are invariably tilted to disadvantage the customer—sometimes transparently, sometimes so mysteriously only a specialist could spot the trick. Large borrowers and depositors can afford to contest these devices. For smaller firms, it is not worth the hassle. This last comment does not mean you should put up with bank sloppiness, overcharges, or rates that are out of line with the competition. These should always be contested immediately. Your protest may not be cost-effective in the short run, but it will help protect your account from future abuse.

Solution C. Minimize your cash balances. Perhaps this strategy should have been mentioned first, not last. It is the most obvious and, once made routine, the easiest solution for many businesses. The key word here is *routine*. If you cannot forecast your cash flows with more than a few minutes' work a day, it may not be worth the effort.

Here is a simple example of how you might assess the value of a small program of cash management. Suppose that with no particular attention to minimizing your cash balance, it averages about $15,000. Inside that sum is $7,000 of cash that could be "squeezed out" with improved forecasting and controls. If your cost of money is 15%, the value of that improvement is worth $1,050 a year.* On the other hand, suppose this improvement takes 30 minutes a day of your accountant's time; and his time, fully loaded for overhead, costs you $12 an hour. The annual cost is $1,500, and the saving of $1,050 is not justified.

Now suppose that with a subprogram on your micro-computer, and minor changes in your operating routine, your secretary can manage your cash in less than 12 minutes a day or an hour a week. Now your cost is down to $400 a year, and the improvement more than pays its way.

In the real world a cost/benefit analysis will seldom be so simple. It is always possible, however, to make some quantitative estimate of the impacts of a change; and this estimate should be prepared. Do not lose sight of the qualitative benefits of better cash control. A beady eye on the cash box will often bring to light problems and opportunities you would not otherwise have noticed. Many businesses practice tight cash control without regard to its cost, realizing intuitively that this is simply part of good management. I will not fault them.

The basic techniques of cash management are mostly common sense, but there are many tricks and helpful devices in this specialized financial discipline. Your library will have at least one book on this subject. *Cash Management* by Mary C. Driscoll is a good text,† though any recently published book on the subject will teach you all you need to know, and then some. In an evening's reading you can easily absorb the book I just recommended. Unless you already know the subject thoroughly, this evening's read will pay you handsome dividends for many years to come. Now to the second reason why businesspeople like to see a large cash balance.

*Your "opportunity cost" of capital, the rate you can earn on additional capital employed, may be double or even triple a mere 15%. In this case, your analysis should reflect the higher figure.
†Published by John Wiley & Sons, New York, N.Y., 1983.

Purpose: To Show an Attractive Balance Sheet

Before proposing any solutions, I want to point out that this purpose is usually misguided. Admittedly there is a long-standing prejudice in favor of financial statements which show substantial free cash balances. Presumably these firms can pay their bills. This notion is as simplistic as it is popular. A firm's ability to pay its bills after the date of its balance sheet will rely almost entirely on its net cash flows and access to credit after that date. Cash in the bank on December 31 will have been spent several times over by mid-March.

Let us look at specific situations. Take a company with no debt and a large cash balance. Yes, it is probably highly creditworthy, but not because of the cash balance. It is creditworthy, among other reasons, because it has no debt. The cash balance merely indicates that the owners have no immediate need for excess funds; or perhaps the cash is there to cover a large dividend, declared and paid the next day.

Now take a company that borrows short-term to inflate its cash on hand ($000):

	Before new debt	*After new debt*
Cash	1	101
Other current assets	100	100
Total current assets	101	201
Short-term bank debt	0	100
Accounts payable	50	50
Total current liabilities	50	150

Before the new debt, our company had a Current Ratio (Current Assets to Current Liabilities) of 2:1, which is considered very sound. After the new debt, its Current Ratio had fallen precipitously to 1.3:1. The Current Ratio is a key test of a firm's financial health and liquidity. In this example the "window dressing," as it is called, of more cash in fact results is a marked deterioration of the firm's financial condition as measured by the key ratio! Arithmetically, as long as the Current Ratio is above the integer one, it can only improve by *reducing* cash to *pay off* short-term debt, with the ancillary benefit of improved earnings due to lower interest expense.

There is a way around this arithmetic dead end: borrow long-term and deposit the proceeds of the loan short-term. Your Current Ratio does indeed improve, and you now show a healthy cash balance. But this is too silly to warrant consideration. You should borrow long-term only to finance a long-term requirement, typically fixed assets, not a cash balance. To do otherwise would needlessly incur the higher expense of long-term debt as compared to short-term debt.

Solution. All this notwithstanding, there is an important kernel of truth in the old prejudice for cash balances: they are an indicator, only an indicator, of liquidity and prudence. By referring back to the principle established earlier—that cash and credit are fungible—you can glimpse the solution: establish a line of credit that is entirely or largely not drawn down. A prominent footnote to your balance sheet describes the availability.

This availability is better than cash:

1. It cannot, normally, disappear overnight.

2. It proves that a lender has analyzed your business and pronounced it creditworthy.

3. It is much less expensive than maintaining a cash balance. The commitment fee on the unused portion of your line should not be more than 1%–1.25%.

4. It shows you are a smart executive: you have provided for unforeseen events in the most cost-effective manner.

In my capacities as a private investor and head of household, I have substantial debt obligations, no regular income, and no more cash than is in my wallet. At the same time, I have unused lines of personal credit sufficient to meet any conceivable demands for payment. These credit lines cost me a few hundred dollars a year, but they are a bargain at the price. Without these backup lines of credit, I would have to maintain sizable cash balances at my banks to meet unexpected outlays. The cost of such balances in interest and opportunities forgone would far exceed my present expense of the commitment fees. Most solvent businesses can employ the same strategy.

Almost certainly some of you who use this system will encounter antediluvian creditors who are shocked that you have little or no cash in the bank. You then must explain that cash and credit are fungible, and you show them a copy of your standby credit agreement with the bank. The longer the notice period, the time period required for the lender to notify you that he wishes to cancel the credit, the better. If you have to pay ⅛% or ¼% more in commitment fee for a notice period of one year rather than three months, do so.

Purpose: To Keep the Bank Happy With a Large Cash Balance

Solution. Don't. As pointed out in Chapter 10 under Compensating Balances, the bank can always borrow money more cheaply than you can. If your bank makes weak protestations to the effect that it would like to see larger balances to cover the cost of your account, be sympathetic and do nothing. Your balances are probably right about where they should be.

When your account officer puts on a very severe face, says that an analysis of your account shows a loss for the bank, and demands that you increase your balances, she is probably serious. In this case you should piously protest that you certainly do not expect the bank to run your account at a loss. Propose a change over to direct compensation for services on a fee basis. This will flush out the quarry, and your account officer has no place to hide. If your account really is unprofitable, the bank will agree to handle it on a fee basis, and you can compare the fees it charges with those of other banks. If it is bluffing, it will back down and, under protest, accept your existing level of balances.

Purpose: A Cash Reserve for Emergencies

Solution. Since cash and credit are fungible, this need is accommodated by a substantial standby line of unused credit, as discussed fully three pages back. Look upon this credit facility no differently than you would a basic insurance policy. In exchange for a modest premium (commitment fee) you protect yourself against unforeseeable events. And, as just pointed out, the standby credit confers other advantages for which you pay nothing.

Some banks will still try to convince you that there is no substitute for a cash reserve (cash balance) in your deposit account, and they will be delighted to lend you the money to maintain it. In fact, a recent mailing from my bank in New Jersey urged me to preserve my valuable cash balance with the bank, pay my bills by drawing on my credit line, and thereby conserve my liquidity! In other words, I should leave my cash in a noninterest-bearing deposit and then borrow it back from the bank under another name. Simple arithmetic destroys this sophistry. Yet, as the Southern Methodist University study proves, it has a deep appeal to many of us. Do not be fooled.

Bear in mind that no matter how much idle cash you leave in your bank account, you are *not* building up "brownie points" to use in the future. The windfall in cost-free funds to the bank goes directly into its current P&L. It will not at a later time cede back to you that historical profit through a lower interest rate or any other concession. Well, some institutions might, but I've never seen it happen.

19.

RAISING EQUITY AND VENTURE CAPITAL

As pointed out earlier, the subject of this book is credit—that is, borrowed funds, not equity capital. Yet most firms will find that at one time or another their ability to raise borrowed money is limited or even nil because their equity base is too small to support more debt. It would be unfair not to give these firms guidance in this other area of finance.

Assume you need more equity to get started or to expand. You have pursued the obvious sources: a second mortgage on your home, friends, relations, and business acquaintances. Whatever you have been able to gather is not enough. This does not reflect poorly on your business prospects. Very few entrepreneurs have wealthy friends with bottomless pockets.

The Role of Venture Capitalists

So now you must turn to the professionals who invest in relatively small or untried enterprises. They are called "venture capitalists," and this name accurately describes their function. They invest their own or other investors' funds in equity shares and/or equity-related debt, thereby absorbing much of the risk that the commercial lenders have been unwilling to shoulder. If the new infusion of equity capital is sufficient, the lenders will reconsider your application.

In practice almost all venture capitalists, if they are willing to invest in your company, will also assist you in developing a corresponding increase in loan capital. Generally they have excellent contacts in the credit markets and a highly refined sense of how to "structure" a deal so that for any given infusion of equity the resulting increase in debt capacity is optimized. Unless you yourself are a sophisticated borrower, the venture capitalist will probably take over the entire corporate finance area, subject to your understanding and agreement. Be suspicious of a financier who evidences little concern for your understanding and agreement. You don't want a major partner in your business who ignores your position; worse, without your participation he may maneuver to increase his financial advantage and control beyond what you originally contemplated.

Now, if it has not been obvious from the outset, you should realize that in seeking professional investors you will have to cede a substantial amount of equity in your business as well as some control over decision-making. These concessions will vary, but they are always present to a greater or lesser degree. Most entrepreneurs dislike this. Many dislike it so intensely they refuse it, and they decide to "go it alone."

Experienced observers in the investment and financial communities are unanimous when reacting to the "go it alone" decision: don't do it. Assuming you need (not just want) additional equity capital and you have found willing investors, always bring them in if their conditions and personalities are acceptable. Experts invariably remark that it is far, far better to own 50% of a well-capitalized, growing business than 100% of one failing for want of adequate funding.

Any venture capitalist worth his salt will increase dramatically the likelihood of your achieving the former outcome. Not only will he help you create a proper capital structure, he will provide you with industry intelligence, introductions to new customers, financial reports and controls appropriate to your business, and a sophisticated review of your strategic plans and decisions. At the other extreme, he might screw up your business to a fare-thee-well, but this outcome is so rare that it is hardly worth considering. You reduce its likelihood to a near-impossibility by talking with the owners of other businesses your investor has already financed.

When you do not accept a venture capitalist and things go poorly, you then have to return to him for the investment you originally rejected. Your enterprise will be tainted by failure rather than enhanced by the prospect of success. Any investment you can negotiate now will be on terms much less favorable than you could have obtained at the outset.

Please realize that only about one proposal in 30 is ever accepted for financing by a venture capitalist. So if your project is good enough to attract an offer, almost certainly you should take it. Do not pine because someone else will profit from your ideas and hard work. After all, you will benefit too, and your benefit will be increased greatly by the investor's participation.

Venture capital firms are rarely interested in small investments, say under $100,000, or companies with sales of less than $1 million, unless their prospects for growth in revenues and profits are extraordinary. Neither are they often interested in inventions requiring further research, development, and engineering. They prefer companies and products that are already selling and are proven successes but lack the capital to exploit their markets.

Not only are embryonic projects difficult to evaluate and the riskiest category, they demand a disproportionate amount of time and effort to bring to fruition. A typical venture capitalist will receive dozens of proposals a week. Obviously he will focus on those which are the most advanced, best thought-out and presented, and most easily exploited for rapid earnings. He works on probabilities, and your project must appeal to his criteria.

Finding and Approaching Venture Capitalists

The smaller your project or the further it is in time from a successful launch, the more spectacular the ultimate payoff has to be. Hence, unlike your presentations to a commercial banker, your sales and profit forecasts to a venture capitalist might have to grow exponentially if they are to attract any interest. When your forecasts show only unsupported numbers that climb into the blue sky, however, they will be laughed at and thrown away. So you must develop a balance between caution and wild optimism, but partial to optimism. Earlier chapters on the loan application, ratcheted up for this new purpose, are a guide.

When you submit your entire business plan package to a venture capital firm, it has to be comprehensive. You should review all chapters and appendices in this book on preparing a loan application to ensure that you have covered everything.

You may have developed highly sophisticated graphs, formulae, and tables to prove your certain success, and that's good. Include them, but make sure the numbers feed directly into conventional financial statements. These latter are the documents the venture capitalist always understands and uses to help make his decision.

When your story on markets and marketing is not knowledgeable and persuasive, automatic rejection is a certainty. If an investor sees a weakness in materials handling, he can ensure it is corrected. If he sees a promoter who does not understand his market, however, he will not proceed, for this is a deficiency too basic for an investor to correct.

The principal reference books for sources of venture capital in the United States are:

> *The Corporate Finance Sourcebook*, published by the Zehring Company, Wilmette, IL. It lists 600 venture capital firms.

> *Pratt's Guide to Venture Capital Sources*, published by Venture Economics, Inc. Wellesley Hills, MA. It lists almost 1,000 firms, though generally with somewhat less detail.

Businesses with strong foreign connections might examine:

> *Venture Economic's Guide to European Venture Capital Sources*, also published by Venture Economics.

These are specialized and expensive publications, so you will not find them in small libraries. Most universities with a business school will have them, as will major libraries in larger towns and cities. Small libraries plugged into computerized search systems can quickly identify which nearby, larger libraries have these reference works.

Most firms should peruse both of the first two reference works, since each has some advantages over the other. *Pratt's Guide* provides excellent introductory material on the venture capital industry, terminology, how to approach investors, and so forth. Since they are updated annually, be sure to use an edition no older than last year's.

The descriptions of investors given in these books are based only on information submitted, so they may be inaccurate or incomplete. Nonetheless, they are generally informative and reliable. Here is a composite example of the kind of listing they contain:

XYZ Venture Capital Corp.
1234 Enterprise Blvd.
Anywhere, USA

Investment committee officers:

James Fiero, Chairman
Gale Dale, Sr. Vice President
Carl Steiner, Analyst

Officer to contact: any of the above

Type of financing or service offered: 1st, 2nd, and 3rd stage equity financings only

Minimum investment: $250,000

Industry preferences: retailing, wholesale distribution, consumer goods, light manufacturing

Preferred size of investment: $½ to $2 million

Geographical preference: Mountain states

Data required: 3 years history + full prospectus

Year of establishment: 1975

Funds under management: $14 million

Funds available for investment: $5 million

Deals done in last fiscal year: 4

Investments in last fiscal year: $3.2 million

As is evident from the example above, most of the listings will be eliminated from your consideration on the grounds of size, industry specialization, or geography. You will be left with perhaps 50 prospects. Like the investors, your time is valuable, and you work with probabilities.

Sending a full-scale business plan of 50 or 100 pages to 50 candidates would be expensive and time consuming for both parties. Instead, prepare a summary proposal of three or four pages, noting that the full business plan is available on request. Clearly this summary must be exceptionally well prepared; for unless you have been able to obtain a personal endorsement from a respected go-between, it will be your only opportunity to arouse the investor's interest.

As in applying for debt capital to commercial lenders, you must allow for a lengthy period of review, delays, further questions, and negotiations. Six months from initial contact to availability of funds would be minimum, 12 months a more conservative time-frame.

Assuming you are successful in raising capital, you will find another time-frame that differs from most commercial lending. A venture capitalist will usually become your partner for a period of 5–10 years. When policy disagreements or personality clashes develop, you cannot shed your investor and walk across the street to find another. You are "married," for better or for worse. Hence you must use great care when selecting your partner.

By the way, even if you get a commitment of, say, $5 million, you are unlikely to see it all at once (unless its purpose is simply to retire other financial obligations already outstanding). Your funds will be parceled out to you bit by bit, with the availability of each installment dependent on your having met certain clearly defined goals. Don't be angered by this restriction. It is standard practice and is designed to protect both parties from unproductive outlays.

Venture Capital Clubs

In addition to the reference books cited, there is a parallel and more personal way to find investors, and that is to contact one of the venture capital clubs now active throughout the United States. These clubs typically bring together venture capitalists, entrepreneurs, investment bankers, middlemen, promoters, and other interested specialists. They meet every month or two and are cauldrons of ideas and opportunities.

You cannot find them in the phone book, and new ones are springing up all the time. To find the venture capital club nearest you, write to:

> Association of Venture Capital Clubs, 196 North St., PO Box 1333, Stamford, CT, 06904; *and* Venture Capital Club Monthly, 805 Third Avenue, New York, NY, 10022.

Both organizations assured me they will answer your questions and will send you a free sample of their periodicals.

The clubs are essentially "networking" groups. Their charges to attend a meeting range from $5–$25, and that is little enough to pay when you are seeking a substantial investment. Most give each participant an opportunity to speak to the group and explain his interests. The meetings are definitely "hands on" affairs. Although most of the members are experienced players, the clubs welcome novices.

SBIC's, MESBIC's, and Other Government Programs

Small Business Investment Companies (SBIC's) are privately owned and operated venture capital firms which have been licensed and partly financed by the Small Business Administration (SBA) to provide equity capital and long-term loans to small companies. The SBA's definition of "small" is much larger than you might imagine: a net worth not over $6 million and profits after tax not over $2 million. All but a handful of this book's readers will fit that definition.

There are about 400 active SBIC's, and they are to be found throughout the nation. Those nearest you can be identified in the first two reference books cited earlier in this chapter, by writing to the National Association of Small Business Investment Companies, 618 Washington Building, Washington, DC, 20005, and by contacting your regional SBA field office.

Because of the way they are financed, SBIC's prefer to provide loan rather than equity capital; the loans are convertible into common stock, or the SBIC takes stock warrants, or some other device is used to share in the hoped-for success of the enterprise. Without direct equity investment in cash, an SBIC loan financing would be unacceptable to entrepreneurs whose firms have no further capacity to service debt. On the other hand, SBIC's often do make equity investments, in cash, up front, and their loan capital can usually be subordinated to other debt, thereby providing a "cushion" for the conventional lender. Some SBIC's are as sophisticated and innovative as the best of the "pure" venture capital firms. Hence, as a generalization, those seeking capital should approach them and deal with them in the way described earlier for other venture capitalists.

MESBIC's, or Minority Enterprise Small Business Investment Companies, are a variation of SBIC's; they limit their financing to firms owned at least 51% by socially or economically disadvantaged minorities. These businesses may require greater-than-average managerial support, which the MESBIC's also provide. The American Association of MESBIC's at 915 Fifteenth Street, NW, Washington, DC, 20005, will advise you which members operate in your area; the reference books already cited list some of the more active ones; and your regional SBA field office will have a list.

There are numerous governmental equity finance vehicles below the federal level. Contact your state, regional, or local government offices concerned with economic development to identify them. Appendix F, Sources of Governmental Assistance, goes into this subject in more detail. It also discusses the SBA's regular loan programs for small businesses.

AFTERWORD

The relationship between author and reader is reciprocal, like that between lender and borrower. If you notice ways in which this book could be improved, any recent developments not adequately covered, or some good illustrative stories, drop me a line, c/o Walker and Company, 720 Fifth Avenue, N.Y., N.Y. 10019. My own experience can sample only a fraction of the credit transactions that take place—or fail to take place—every day. Constant feedback from the marketplace, beyond my own activities, is essential to the value of this book.

Please don't ignore the Appendices. They are integral parts of this book. The main text omitted some subjects for the sake of a logical progression. The Appendices explain more of the mechanics, the nuts and bolts. Few businesspersons would proceed on principles and guidelines alone.

Several of my friends—some of them borrowers, some lenders—read the book in manuscript. They all objected to my frequent recommendations that the reader research some specialized point at the library: they said a useful book should not admit incompleteness. Books on business, however, take up several feet of shelf space even in a small library. This one volume cannot include all that information. You have read this book, which proves you are eager to learn, so why not go on elsewhere to learn more?

Bankers who read the manuscript objected to some negative remarks about bankers (which, in fact, are few and mild). Well, bankers *are* human: they make mistakes; they have prejudices, just like any other professional group; and some have gone to jail for theft and fraud. It would be dishonest to pretend otherwise. On the other hand, I have also insisted that the great majority of bankers are competent and rigorously honest.

You will notice that I have touched on the same subject in several different places and sometimes repeated myself. The first practice arises because a subject such as accounting cannot be confined to one chapter called Accounting. Accounting pervades most parts of business activity, and so it has pervaded many chapters of this book. Further, preparing a loan application, negotiating a loan, and nourishing a fruitful credit relationship do not take place in a rigid sequence. It's like designing a complex bit of machinery: you often go back to the beginning and then make adjustments all over the place.

The repetitions arise for different reasons. Some mistakes in business are so frequent and obvious that their persistence is confounding. Hence I've given the same advice more than once, whenever I felt that a point needed special emphasis or a reminder in a different context.

An author should state his prejudices. I've talked at length and as objectively as I could about selecting lenders. Yet there is a subjective element here that is hard to describe. Lenders are not abstractions. They vary from one loan officer or branch to the next, so much so that selecting a financial institution is sometimes like rolling the dice. Nevertheless, you like to have the odds on your side.

Here is how I perceive the odds. Look for a long-established bank or finance house, one that has been at the same street address for many years, preferably decades. It may not have the latest gimmicks or the lowest prices. On the other hand, once you become its customer, it is more likely to take care of you than some jumped-up rival recently taken over by a holding company.

Old lenders usually have long memories. New lenders often haven't been around long enough to remember their customers' names.

I like this personal observation by an old hand, Robert Wilkes, executive vice president of First Jersey National Bank: "If you find a good banker, stay with him and pray that he doesn't leave or get transferred." For "banker" read "account officer," whether he works for a small, local leasing company or Morgan Guaranty Trust. Three times out of four he will give you a better shake than a stranger.

Despite my partiality to the older credit houses, I should add that the new lender on the block has to be more aggressive so that he can win enough volume to cover his overheads. Initially his prices will be better and his loan terms more flexible—until he achieves that minimum volume. Then his services will fall into line with the competition. Hence, if you are a first-time borrower, the latest entry to the market may be your best choice.

APPENDICES

APPENDICES

APPENDIX A. CHECKLIST OF
APPLICATION REQUIREMENTS

Earlier chapters discussed in detail the goals and qualitative requirements of a loan application (Chapters 6 and 7) as well as how to prepare the pro forma financial statements (Chapters 2 and 8). The purpose of this Appendix is to bring that earlier discussion into a completed application, an application suited to your particular situation.

As pointed out in Chapter 7, the length of your application and degree of detail are partly questions of judgment. By the same token, the specific subjects you include depend on your assessment of your individual circumstances. Production processes using toxic or flammable substances require permits and safety measures which must be dealt with in the application or at least in an appendix to it. A retail store may require no more than a $10 trading license, hardly worth mentioning.

The application itself demands no rigid format or order of materials. The tabulation following is not intended to mandate a progression, since what is crucial, important, or ancillary varies from business to business. The rules of thumb are:

1. Present comprehensive material first, so the reader can put later specific subjects into perspective.

2. Progress from the more important to the less important.

3. Relegate backup material to appendices where they will not interrupt the flow of your story.

That much said, for most applications the sequence of subjects as presented in the following pages should be about right.

A *covering letter* should describe the nature of your business, the project to be financed, and the amount and kind of funding you are seeking. This capsule statement should be no more than two paragraphs long. If the contact person in your firm is at a different address or phone number from those shown on the letterhead, this should be noted. Do not fail to show your title and sign and date the letter. These last points are self-evident, I know, but yours would not be the first-ever application to have omitted them.

If the legal name of the business is not the name on your letterhead, specify the name of the borrowing entity. For example, "Western Union" does not borrow money; "The Western Union Telegraph Company" is the legal entity that does.

The table of contents will permit the reader to look up quickly any specific subject. It should identify the page numbers for each subject. A sample follows:

CONTENTS	*Comments & References*
History of the Business	Essential. Appendix A
Description of the Project	Essential. Appendix A
Summary of the Financing	Essential. Appendix A
Market Analysis	Essential. Appendix A; Chapters 2 and 7
Ownership and Management	Essential. Appendix A; Chapters 7 and 11
Technical and Engineering	Optional. Appendix A
Legal Considerations	Essential. Appendix A
Employee Relations	Desirable. Appendix A
Pro Forma Financial Statements	Essential. Appendix A; Chapters 2, 7 and 8
Historical Financial Statements	Essential for all existing businesses. Appendix A
Personal Financial Statements	Usually required. Appendix A
Breakeven Analysis	Often desirable. Appendix A, Appendix E
Discussion of Risks	Usually essential. Appendix A
Real Estate	If required to support credit. Appendix A
References	Necessary for a new or small business. Appendix A

CONTENTS (continued)   *Comments & References*

Letters from Suppliers and   Depends. See Appendix A
    Customer

Industry Comparisons   Usually desirable. Appendix A

Environmental Considerations   When a factor, essential.
                     Appendix A

New Product Development   Usually necessary. Appendix A

Accounting and Controls   Essential, if only a paragraph.
                     Appendix A

Insurance   Essential. Appendix A

Critical Advantages   Essential, if your project is
                     major. Appendix A

Background Documentation   Essential to have on file.
                     Appendix A; Chapters 2 and 7

A history of your business will give enough background to put subsequent material into perspective. The year of establishment, number of employees, and recent growth in sales and profits are appropriate to describe here. If you are starting a new business, you substitute here a section entitled "Origin of the Enterprise." It might say, "In 1986 three chemists at Exxon Research Corporation began meeting on weekends to discuss an entirely new approach to the synthesis of certain rare hydrocarbons. Since Exxon was not interested in pursuing this opportunity, they resigned and . . ."

A description of the project should follow logically from the previous section, aided by a transitional sentence or paragraph. This present section contains an extended textual and qualitative description of the project (or expansion, improvement, consolidation, whatever). It should be interlaced with summary statistical and financial data to give the reader an overview of the enterprise and a feeling for the magnitude of the project. Always try to set out key data in tabular form rather than incorporating the numbers into your text. *Avoid:* we forecast sales during the first three years at $50,000 in 1986, $100,000 in 1987, and $200,000 in 1988. *Use instead:*

	1986	*1987*	*1988*
Forecast sales (in $000)	*$50*	*$100*	*$200*

Other key information included here would be the location of the new facility, size, number of additional staff, identification of major customers, and expected profitability. Fit into your text your *critical* advantages, two or three factors which you are counting on to ensure the success of your project against the competition (e.g., a patent, an exclusive distributorship, a breakthrough in cost reduction or product design, or a unique location). Later in your application you will support these claims with convincing detail. After all, only one business in a thousand has more than two or three advantages over its competitors, so stress here these critical assets. Everything else required, such as a good system of cost control, can be described later on, simply to prove you have covered all the bases.

A *summary of the financing* might be appropriate here. I am partial to setting out early on: 1) the amount of the credit request; 2) the purpose of the loan; and 3) when it will be repaid. The same information will be provided later in the financial schedules and in greater detail; however, a lender likes an overview of her participation early on so that she can assess the rest of the material in relation to that commitment. Furthermore, your lender likes to see that from the beginning you realize that the name of the game is to pay back the money. In many credit applications this is added as an afterthought or forgotten completely, which leaves a poor impression.

This section should describe the major terms and conditions you are proposing, for example: secured by a lien on receivables acceptable to the bank plus finished goods inventory, maximum advances of 75% of the former and 50% of the latter; 30-day additional credit of $150,000 required from mid-November to mid-December to finance Christmas peak sales. Or: moratorium on principal repayments requested for initial 6 months of loan to allow for completion of fabrication (3 months), testing, crating, and delivery (1/2 month), inspection and acceptance by customer (1/2 month), receipt of payment (1 month), and contingency (1 month). You may reasonably request any special condition you want, as long as it is conservative and reflects the underlying economic activity in your business.

A *market analysis* should now follow if your business is, like almost all businesses, dependent on successful marketing in a highly competitive environment. The minimum requirements here are estimates of the total size of your market, the strengths and weaknesses of your competition (price, quality, service, etc.), your strengths and weaknesses, your forecast market share, and the duration of your advantages.

Speaking only to the last point: remember hula hoops; you may have been the low-cost producer; when the fad passed, that was no advantage. Remember Woolworth's and A&P, the retail food giant. Forty years ago they had the best locations across the country. Most of these locations are now abandoned.

It is seldom an easy matter to assess a market, its size, your actual and/or potential share of it, and its continuance. Yet you have to try or else admit ignorance of the main determinant of the success of your enterprise. Larger businesses, especially, hire marketing consultants and researchers to perform surveys, studies, and analyses. In my experience these commissions are usually costly and inferior substitutes for hard work and careful thinking on the part of the client firms. *You* can stand on the sidewalk and count pedestrian traffic. *You* can research Bureau of Census data, and *you* can look up published material on your industry in *Predicasts F&S Index* and in such sources as the example in Appendix B.*

Assuming you are not a one-armed paperhanger and have a staff, ask an assistant to develop the data you need. Advantages: 1) costs less; 2) quicker; 3) trains the aide; 4) informs you as to his ability to strike out on his own; and 5) you understand the results and their limitations, since your firm has done the work.

Unfortunately, I have to admit that most lenders will accord less weight to your work than they would to a report from an "independent expert." To overcome this prejudice your work must be well-prepared, unbiased, and convincing. Your explanation of why you decided to do the study yourself should be equally convincing.

A review of ownership and management is essential. Chapter 7 describes how personal backgrounds should be presented from a strategic point of view. In this section I would suggest summary biogra-

---

*Predicasts F&S Index is published monthly by Predicasts, Inc., Cleveland, OH. The monthly reports are incorporated into annual volumes which go back many years. This reference work provides a comprehensive listing of articles appearing in some 1,200 domestic and foreign periodicals, for instance, *Rubber & Plastic News, Tea and Coffee Trade Journal, Discount Merchandising.*

Predicasts covers both manufacturing and service industries, and its listings are classified by SIC (Standard Industrial Classification) number initially in large groupings—e.g., Transport Equipment, Financial Services—and then by very specific industries—e.g., 2211 Cotton Broadwoven Fabrics, 73760 Computer Leasing. Each listing provides the source of the article, its title, and a one-line description of the subject. Rare is the researcher who cannot use this source to track down almost everything happening in his industry.

phies, with full biographies of the key players in an appendix. Provide not only the titles of these executives but descriptions of their authority and what they actually *do*. A Controller may be only a clerk/ bookkeeper; in many companies that is all he is. In some companies the Controller is also the Chief Financial Officer, right-hand man to the Chief Executive Officer, and de facto number two in the organiza- tion.

If your organization is complex (or simple, but the lines of authority and interaction complex), this would be a suitable place for an organization chart. Again, set out what really happens, not just titles. I know of a company where the President is a figurehead; in fact he is an inventor. The Chairman of the Board is the executive who determines policy and runs the company on a day-to-day basis.

When you have a Board of Directors and it plays an important role in the business, then its composition and managerial role should be described. Technically, in any corporation the Board bears the ulti- mate legal authority and responsibility for conduct of the company's affairs. In practice, since most corporations are owned by only a few stockholders/executives, the Board often performs only legal formali- ties. In these cases the role of the Board may be ignored, except for such formalities.

Technical, legal, financial, and other advisors should be identified, their roles and qualifications described. This need not be a separate section; you can identify them and include them under other sections such as engineering, management, legal, and so forth.

A *technical or engineering* section is mandatory when these factors are critical to the success of the enterprise. It should be brief and in layman's language. A full discussion should be provided in an appen- dix or referred to as available on request. State the professional credentials of the person(s) on whose say-so any technical conclusions are presented.

Legal matters will frighten lenders if lawsuits have been filed or threatened. Unless these suits are central to the success of the project, I would leave them to the very end, almost as a footnote. Most businesses of any substantial size have one or more lawsuits or threats outstanding. Usually these are "nuisance actions," covered by insur- ance, without merit, or negotiable on reasonable terms. Do not highlight them; bury them at the end of the application. If they do represent a real threat to your business, set out the facts clearly and fairly early on to avoid any impression of attempted concealment.

"Legal matters" can include a wide range of subjects besides lawsuits, most of them routine, and these latter should be covered later on under other headings or in an appendix. (Specific items are mentioned under several different subjects to come.) When a legal problem is not routine, for example, when implementation of your project depends on a favorable ruling by your municipal planning authority, say so up front. Lenders assume you are ready to proceed unless you state otherwise.

This section on legal matters should define the legal status of your enterprise, e.g., incorporated in the State of Delaware (1974) with sales and service branches in Trenton, NJ (1978), and Hartford, CT (1983); corporate offices located at 1234 Market Street, Newark, NJ, since 1975. If your firm is not a corporation, then it is probably a sole proprietorship or a partnership. All three principal types of legal existence have variations, and these should be spelled out so that your lender knows what kind of organization she is dealing with.

When two or more legal entities are involved, each should be described, along with the ownerships and contractual relationships. If the legal relations amongst these entities are complex, then a chart should be included to illustrate the textual explanation.

Employee relations or labor relations should be described if they are important to the success of your business. Usually they are. A pending strike *must* be mentioned. A recent contract establishing a new era of harmony *should* be mentioned. Be careful to be truthful; this is an area your lender probably knows something about. If your employee relations are excellent and staff morale high, say so. It may be your opinion, true, but it is probably also a fact; it is important to your creditor.

Pro forma financial statements are, of course, the very heart of your application. We have gone over the preparation and presentation of the principal ones with great care in Chapters 2, 7, and 8.

Historical financial statements are essential assuming you have a business history. The easiest statements to use are those you filed with your Federal corporate income tax return. Almost certainly these are the statements your lender will request, since she will assume that you have not overstated your profits. Using these financials, however, might create a misleading impression of your business's profitability for three major reasons:

1. Taking advantage of tax concessions, incentives, and loopholes, you drastically reduced your taxable income or even showed a loss! This might have been good business, but it may look

terrible in a loan application. The solution is to recast your financial statements to show in a separate calculation the "true" profitability of your business after all the artificial tax effects have been removed. *Do not* just explain this adjustment in a conversation with your loan officer; it may be forgotten or misremembered. Display the recalculation prominently in your application, carefully identifying it as such.

2. You have made an investment or taken some other action intended to improve your business markedly in the long run, knowing that in the short run it would result in major losses or other unfavorable effects. For example, you bought out your main competitor, paying too much for his obsolete inventories, but knowing that after two years your capture of his market would lead to much greater profits. So, for two years, you suffer from depressed profits or even losses as the excess cost of inventories is reflected in write-offs. Again, *do not* rely on a verbal explanation. Work out the numbers, even if they can only be estimates, show the "true" historical profits of your business without the depressing effects, and present them prominently.

3. You have concealed and understated your profits to evade and/or postpone paying income taxes. This is illegal. If it were not a common practice with profitable, privately owned businesses, I would rail against it. Unfortunately, it is, and so, like adultery and jaywalking, I have to accept it as part of the real world. My reluctant acceptance, however, still leaves you with a most serious problem. You are sitting across from your account officer, trying to convince her how honest you are and, at the same time, you are giving her falsified tax returns. Further, these fraudulent returns undermine, in black and white, the basis for your loan application, since they show your business to be much less profitable than in fact it is.

    In such a dicey matter I cannot provide any certain answer. I don't think there is any. Nevertheless, the problem is so common it must be addessed. My first piece of advice is *do not* include in your application a calculation of how much you have cheated the tax man and how much more profitable your business is than appears on the books. Second, at some time *early on*, when you are alone with your loan officer, explain to her that the real profits were understated by so many thousands of dollars in each of the past three years. An experienced account officer will have heard this before, and she will know what to do. If she is green, she might be horrified, but she will control her indignation and take the matter to her superior. Her superior will know what to do. A common handling of this situation is for the lender to verify through audit or other means that the undisclosed profits and/or values are in fact as you have claimed. The lender may require that there be no future diversion of funds or misstatement of values.

Although banks are required by law to report certain transactions to the authorities, they have no obligation to report suspicion of income tax evasion. I would be very surprised if any banker would notify the IRS under circumstances such as described above.

Use of the same format for financial schedules as presented in Chapter 8, that is, combining your historical and forecast statements to show a chronological continuity, will relieve you of the need to include your historical statements in a separate section. In this case your lender may ask for copies of your tax returns just to verify the number you have presented.

A *breakeven analysis* is almost always helpful when your volume of sales is a major determinant of success. Appendix E explains how to develop and present this analysis.

A *listing and assessment of the risks* of the project and your existing business will prove you are not living on cloud nine, where everything is eternally rosy. This key section should show your business acumen and prudence and what you will do to protect your firm from the vicissitudes of competition and happenchance. Chapter 7 discusses in depth the subject of risk assessment. Although those pages are oriented to quantifying risks and providing for them in your pro forma financial statements, the discussion will indicate how the "risk" section of your application should confront the subject both quantitatively and qualitatively.

It will not suffice to state, as many prospectuses for equity or debt capital do, that the investment "entails a high degree of risk." You have to describe the risks carefully, try to quantify them, and explain how you are going to counter them.

Personal financial statements will be required of your firm's principal owners, guarantors, and members of management whenever personal guarantees are required from them. In most small businesses such guarantees will be required. Your lender will have forms for this purpose, and with the knowledge gained from reading this far, you will have no difficulty in filling out these forms. Once again, be truthful. The major facts of an individual's financial history and current position are usually easy to check out. Guarantees depending on the *income* as well as the *assets* of the guarantor will require evidence of that income. Prior years' personal tax returns will be required.

I might add that there is no advantage to including as assets old automobiles, minor jewelry, or Great Aunt Mary's marble washbasin. Inclusion of such items bespeaks of an effort to "puff up" your net worth; the lender cannot be troubled to value them; and in a distress sale they are likely to realize very little. Bona fide valuables with established market values may be included. Even here, the lender will discount your appraisal sharply, since such assets can easily be sold and removed from the lender's grasp.

If you are confident that your business and new project are solid enough to stand without guarantees, omit this section. Let the lender raise the subject and request the extra security.

Real estate locations and valuations. Real estate or any other major asset to be used as security for the loan, whether owned by your business or external to your business, should be identified as to location, ownership, and currently appraised value. Do not pay a professional appraiser yet. The lender may have his own appraiser and charge you nothing. A local real estate agent will usually provide a good estimate of value at no charge, in the hope of future business. Insist that the valuer have at least 10 years' experience.

Business and Personal References. A character reference from your local clergyman might look good. But if you are starting a new business a strong positive statement from a previous employer as to your business ability and accomplishments will be much better. List names, titles, relationships to you, addresses, and phone numbers. *Always* check with proposed references beforehand to get their assurance that they will give you the kind of reference you want. This is not foolproof, but it is a necessary precaution. As for your own personal credit rating, and your company's, see Chapter 12.

Letters from suppliers and customers. General statements that your suppliers are reliable and your customers like your products are worthless. Get a strong letter of support from your principal supplier and permission to use it saying, and I quote from an actual example, "This is to confirm ABC's total support, including temporary funding, to XYZ in completing the development of the X9876 Widget in the shortest possible time . . . We will provide such engineering assistance and support in the on-going development and marketing of the X9876 Widget as required . . ."

Similar convincing letters from your major customers are also desirable. Even better would be a letter and a firm, irrevocable purchase order covering a substantial portion of your production during the next 12 months.

Favorable industry comparisons. A letter of support from a customer would be of little value to a typical retail shop. Look for industry statistics showing you have above-average sales per square foot (always a key ratio), above-average gross margins, or any other evidence of outstanding management, physical location, layout, and product selection. Sales and value added per employee, when exceptionally high for your industry, are also good selling points, though you should take care that the comparisons are meaningful. Very high sales per employee may mean only that you are an assembly operation, whereas your competitors are fully integrated manufacturers.

Environmental considerations. Excessive noise, bright lights, heavy traffic, sewer discharges, noisome odors, you name it: if you are creating or will create an environmental hazard or nuisance, sooner or later you will have legal or community relations problems. It is very unwise merely to assure yourself that you are in conformity with existing legislation, regulations, and planning guidelines. This will not save you from harassment by angry neighbors and new, more restrictive regulation.

Your loan application should contain a paragraph stating that you have determined your business is not and will not be environmentally objectionable, assuming that you are in an industry with potential problems. Summarize the verifications and steps you have taken. If there is an actual or potential problem, refer to an appendix. In the appendix describe the problem and how you plan to handle it. Make sure your solution is definitive, not just an intention to appeal a court decision.

Now, I agree that the average lender is not going to pester you with questions regarding your effluent disposal. You and I can also agree that in the course of your own planning you will address such matters. The ground has to be covered, and it takes only a few extra minutes to explain in your application that you have done it. This looks good in your application. It proves you are conscientious and thorough.

New products and new product development. If your business requires a continuing flow of new products to remain successful—and very few firms do not—you will want to describe your program for development and/or acquisition of new products and services. While some loans are "one-off" transactions, most are rolled over, increased, or replaced by new loans. (This is what the lender wants to see: the subsequent loans will be more profitable to him, as they will not incur the expense of establishing a new credit.) Further, it often turns out that the first loan is not self-liquidating; new products and investments are required to maintain the health of the enterprise. Don't overemphasize the importance of new products, however; the lender may suspect the real purpose of the loan is to finance untested ideas still in the laboratory.

The typical retail business acquires its new products from a common marketplace, but this section on new products still applies. Explain how you stay abreast of changing tastes in the consumer market. Your chief buyer attends the four most important trade fairs in your industry every year and spends four days every month visiting supplier showrooms. Your sales manager spends two days a month visiting and studying competitors' displays and promotions, seeking new products and new marketing ideas.

Key contracts. Leases, options to buy assets, patent rights, distribution agreements, employment contracts, and firm price quotations are all examples of legal documents which may be essential to the success of your business. When they are, they should be summarized in the application. A critical price and delivery commitment from your major supplier should be reproduced and included as an appendix.

Accounting, reporting, and financial controls. These subjects are naturally dear to the hearts of all lenders. Describe your systems in the main body of the application. If they are complex and important to your line of work, provide a fuller description in a separate appendix. A sample computer printout of your accounts receivable classifying overdue accounts by length of delinquency and size demonstrates you recognize the importance of prompt collections. Examples of your monthly actual results comparing them with budget and showing percentage variances would also be appropriate. If you are starting a new business, include samples of the reports and controls you intend to adopt. Demonstrate that someone in your firm has the technical competence and time to produce these reports or that you have arranged for an outside service to produce them for you. Identify your external auditors and describe the scope of their services.

Insurance coverage. State that you have insurance in effect or have arranged for it to be in effect for all major risks, most obviously, property damage and third-party liability. Your insurance broker will try to sell you every kind of coverage you can possibly need, so you run little chance of not being aware of what you should buy.* State that the premiums for these coverages have been included in your pro forma financial statements. Most businessmen might consider these matters too routine to warrant mention. They are not. They are of the highest importance, and your lender likes to see that you recognize them as such. Adequate insurance decreases the lender's risk.

Critical advantages. Earlier in this appendix I spoke of the importance of highlighting your two or three critical advantages. Please go back over your application now and verify that these points were emphasized clearly in one section or another. Possibly the most important advantage deserved a section all to itself.

Background documents. When your application is completed, organize your backup material so that supporting documentation can be found quickly. These documents would include:

All the worksheets for your financial schedules.

Authorization by your Board, certified by the Secretary of the Corporation, for you to negotiate and conclude a loan agreement, for a new bank account to be opened, and for certain persons to operate it.

All commercial licenses, planning approvals, and evidences of current payments of taxes and compliance with other governmental requirements.

Powers of attorney, if such are necessary.

Background studies, especially anything referred to in the text or the appendices, e.g., a marketing study, government statistics, a technical opinion.

Documents you did not refer to directly, but you feel support your application and arguments. In the course of preparing your application you will have read material that was interesting and potentially useful, but you did not think it important enough to use. File it now for ready reference.

---

*Remember to negotiate the largest deductibles you can tolerate and to obtain corresponding decreases in your premiums. This form of limited self-insurance usually creates the biggest savings of any insurance option available.

APPENDIX B. EXAMPLES OF INDUSTRY RATIOS

The tables below are reproduced from *Financial Studies of the Small Business*, sixth edition.* This reference work can be found in largish libraries. It provides the small businessman an objective basis for comparing his actual or planned results with the average of a large sample of similar businesses. Although the examples given here are for manufacturing industries, service industries are also covered by the book.

Do not be put off by the abbreviations and shorthand style of presentation. After reading the explanatory introduction in the book you will find the tables of much interest and value when assessing your enterprise. Obviously, most of your own ratios will differ somewhat, and some will differ markedly from the averages. By focusing on the largest variances you should be able to identify where your firm has special advantages or shortcomings.

The debt ratios will indicate what are considered typical and acceptable levels of borrowing in your industry in relation to your Total Assets and Net Worth. Note also that Interest Expense is broken out as a separate expense category.

*Published by Financial Research Associates, Inc. P.O. Box 2502, Winter Haven, FL 38880. Reprinted by permission of the publisher.

Manufacturers
Machine Tools & Eq.

Total number of firms reporting	39
Number of firms incorporated	36
Number of firms proprietors	3
Number of firms partnerships	0

BREAKDOWN BY SALES

Total sales (in thousands)	10-100 as a pct of sales	100-250 as a pct of sales	250-500 as a pct of sales	500-1000 as a pct of sales
Net sales	999.99	100.00	100.00	100.00
Cost of sales	999.99	60.85	55.70	71.38
Gross profit	999.99	39.15	44.30	28.62
Officer/executive salaries	999.99	13.96	6.85	5.18
General/administrative exp	999.99	18.57	18.91	11.38
Operating profit	999.99	15.35	12.43	6.76
Interest expense	999.99	1.62	0.93	0.59
Depreciation	999.99	4.83	2.94	1.03
Profit before taxes	999.99	4.35	9.31	5.84

ADDITIONAL OPERATING ITEMS

Labor	999.99	21.74	25.96	9.43
Advertising expense	999.99	0.10	0.53	0.04
Travel expense	999.99	0.42	0.33	0.76
Rent	999.99	2.48	1.19	1.50
Insurance	999.99	2.19	2.44	1.00

RATIOS

Current	9999.9	2.7	1.2	2.7
Quick	9999.9	2.0	0.7	1.6
Current assets/total assets	9999.9	41.4	42.6	86.8
Short term debt/total debt	9999.9	40.2	85.7	86.4
Short term debt/net worth	9999.9	22.0	85.1	43.9
Total debt/net worth	9999.9	84.2	98.9	45.8
Short term debt/total assets	9999.9	19.7	27.0	32.1
Long term debt/total assets	9999.9	22.9	8.1	9.7
Total debt/total assets	9999.9	53.4	56.8	47.7
Sales/receivables	9999.9	7.4	14.1	7.2
Average collection period	9999.	40.	16.	50.
Sales/inventory	9999.9	11.2	9.8	9.8
Sales/total assets	9999.9	1.7	2.0	2.7
Sales/net worth	9999.9	3.0	4.6	3.8
Profit (pretax)/total assets	9999.9	6.9	17.7	15.4
Profit (pretax)/net worth	9999.9	19.6	46.3	13.4

Manufacturers   Overall-Sales $10,000-$1,000,000
Machine Tools & Eq. (continued)

INCOME DATA

	As a pct of net sales
Net sales (gross income)	100.00
Cost of sales	62.44
Gross profit	37.56
Officer/executive salaries	6.85
General/administrative exp.	17.97
Operating profit	9.40
Interest expense	0.84
Depreciation	2.00
Profit before taxes	5.78

ADDITIONAL OPERATING ITEMS

Labor	15.31
Advertising expense	0.10
Travel expense	0.52
Rent	1.91
Insurance	2.10

RATIOS

	Median	Upper quartile	Lower quartile	Units
Current	1.9	3.5	0.9	Times
Quick	1.0	2.9	0.5	Times
Current assets/total assets	56.1	85.2	34.6	Pct
Short term debt/total debt	55.3	97.2	36.5	Pct
Short term debt/net worth	41.4	112.6	12.1	Pct
Total debt/net worth	88.3	229.3	25.4	Pct
Short term debt/total assets	27.3	47.8	13.3	Pct
Long term debt/total assets	10.8	48.4	0.3	Pct
Total debt/total assets	55.4	76.0	22.4	Pct
Sales/receivables	7.2	18.2	5.3	Times
Average collection period	30.	58.	14.	Days
Sales/inventory	9.8	28.8	4.1	Times
Sales/total assets	2.1	2.7	1.5	Times
Sales/net worth	3.7	5.8	2.6	Times
Profit (pretax)/total assets	13.6	26.4	-3.4	Pct
Profit (pretax)/net worth	31.9	62.8	-7.5	Pct

Manufacturers
Plastics

All Sizes
Total Assets $10000-$250000

Total number of firms reporting	28
Number of firms incorporated	27
Number of firms proprietors	0
Number of firms partnerships	1

ASSETS

Current assets	As a pct of current assets	As a pct of total assets
Cash	8.04	4.48
Accounts receivables	53.08	29.29
Inventories	19.19	11.92
Other current assets	0.20	0.17

Fixed assets	As a pct of fixed assets	As a pct of total assets
Land, buildings, lease- hold improvements	0.0	0.0
Equipment	100.00	32.09
Other fixed assets	0.0	0.0

LIABILITIES & CAPITAL

Current liabilities	As a pct of current liabilities	As a pct of total liabilities
Accounts payable/trade	35.64	27.74
Short term bank loans	8.69	3.40
Other current debt	44.32	21.92

Long term debt	As a pct of long term debt	As a pct of total liabilities
Mortgages payable	0.0	0.0
Long term bank loans	0.0	0.0
Stockholder loans (due to owners)	0.0	0.0
Other long term debt	0.0	0.0

Manufacturers
Plastics (continued)

All Sizes
Total Assets $10000-$250000

INCOME DATA

	As a pct of net sales
Net sales (gross income)	100.00
Cost of sales	67.04
Gross profit	32.96
Officer/executive salaries	8.92
Other general/administrative expenses	11.58
Operating profit	8.88
Interest expense	1.11
Depreciation	2.08
Profit before taxes	5.90

RATIOS

	Median	Upper quartile	Lower quartile	Units
Current	2.1	4.0	1.5	Times
Quick	1.8	2.9	0.7	Times
Current assets/total assets	63.9	81.8	55.0	Pct
Short term debt/total debt	80.9	100.0	43.6	Pct
Short term debt/net worth	50.3	120.3	17.4	Pct
Total debt/net worth	90.7	173.2	24.2	Pct
Short term debt/total assets	29.3	47.1	16.2	Pct
Long term debt/total assets	6.8	28.3	0.0	Pct
Total debt/total assets	53.0	80.4	29.6	Pct
Sales/receivables	7.9	10.1	6.2	Times
Average collection period	44.	57.	35.	Days
Sales/inventory	12.9	27.8	6.3	Times
Sales/total assets	2.5	3.7	1.6	Times
Sales/net worth	5.4	8.0	2.9	Times
Profit (pretax)/total assets	15.5	26.3	0.5	Pct
Profit (pretax)/net worth	31.8	43.9	13.6	Pct

APPENDIX C. CALCULATING AND COMPARING RATES OF INTEREST

Calculating and comparing rates of interest is simple when the rates are based only on a fixed principal amount outstanding (putting aside rather technical matters such as whether the creditor bases his interest charge on a 360-day or a 365-day year). If credit is in the form of a lease with fixed monthly amounts payable over five years, with the first and last months' payments deposited in advance, with the lessor assuming all the tax advantages, and with "skip payments," determining the true rate of interest can become extremely difficult. A full discussion of this problem would require almost another book, replete with financial tables, complex formulae, and highly technical explanations. Nevertheless, I can summarize here the basic principles, recommend tactics, give some practical examples, and suggest other resources for those who wish to delve more deeply.

The essential principle to grasp is that the true rate of interest to you is always the result of only two variables: the amounts of money available—whether in or out—and when they are available. This concept is neatly summed up in the phrase "the time value of money." That is, a dollar received today is worth more than a dollar received tomorrow because you can earn interest on it for a day. Thus the terms and conditions of a credit which affect the amounts and timing of monies available will also affect the rate of interest to you.

Do not be misled by terminology. Origination fees, finance charges, maintenance charges, discounted loans, and dozens of other phrases all can—and generally do—affect the rate of interest. As far as you are concerned, however, and *for this purpose*, one lender's finance charge is no different from another's rate of interest. You do not care what charges he includes in your cost: he can include tickets to the firemen's ball if he wants to, and call it a closing fee. You need to know only the effect on your cost of money.

The phrase "for this purpose" in the preceding paragraph was emphasized because when it comes to negotiations, your cash needs, or the presentation of your financial statements, there might be very important differences. For example, the lender might be willing to reduce his requirement for compensating balances but rigidly opposed to reducing his nominal rate of interest. Again, you may have restrictions on incurring additional debt, but none on leasing equipment. Considerations such as these may be material, even deciding. They do not influence how you calculate your cost of money.

To illustrate this point: suppose we have two lenders and one includes his cost of setting up or originating the loan (title searches, legal fees, etc.) as part of his general overhead to be covered from the difference between his interest income and his cost of money. The other lender sees them as out-of-pocket costs directly attributable to the transaction at hand, and he wants to recover them immediately. Moreover, the second lender insists on a compensating balance of 15% of the loan drawn down (and we will assume 100% of the loan is drawn down for one year). Here is how the pricing of the loans might look to the borrower:

	First Lender	Second Lender
Gross amount of loan	$100.00	$100.00
Origination fee	—	(2.00)
Compensating balance	—	(15.00)
Net cash to borrower	$100.00	$83.00
Nominal interest rate	15.0%	14.0%
True interest rate	15.0%	16.9%

In this example the first lender's cost to you would be a true rate of interest of 15%. The second lender's would be 16.9% (14% ÷ the actual availability of funds of $83). Again, you do not care how the lenders charge for their services. Your only concern is the net cost to you expressed as the true interest rate, directly comparable between these two sources of credit.

In the case of a loan which simply carries interest at an agreed rate on the balance outstanding, like a personal credit card balance and the examples above, the calculation is usually simple. You adjust for any compensating balance requirements, special fees, and miscellaneous charges, and you calculate the rate. If interest and the repayment of principal are lumped together in equal and fixed monthly payments, as is the case in a typical mortgage, without consulting special financial tables or using the appropriate mathematical formula, you cannot determine the rate. Ask your account officer what rate she has used. Explain that you want the annual percentage rate or "APR."

Most loan officers will provide this on request; usually it is quoted right up front. If your loan officer hedges, do not be put off. If she cannot answer your question, insist on talking to her supervisor or the person who can. When you get the APR, then ask to see its application to the net amount of borrowed funds to be made available to you. With tables or formulae your informant should be able to "prove out" the rate. If she cannot or will not, something is fishy. Persist. Ask for photocopies of the tables and calculations and write down the methodology. Even if you yourself cannot reconstruct the calculation, you should have enough documentation for a third party to do it for you.

The APR, by the way, may or may not be your "true rate of interest," for a variety of reasons. It will, however, show you how the lender calculates his charges to you; then you can make adjustments to see the picture from *your* point of view. Ideally, after a lot of comparing of notes and argument, the lender and you will agree that some particular rate reflects both your cost and the gross income to the lender.

If the APR quoted cannot be proved out because of other, noninterest factors, ask your lender to try to include estimates in the equation and work out a new APR on that basis. She may not think it properly represents the bank's point of view; but if the bank is prepared to lend you money, why should it not be prepared to help you figure out the effects of this loan on your business from your side of the table? A compensating balance requirement, for example, represents a real cost to you, as well as a cash reserve which you can use when required. Both parties understand that. So why not quantify the cost and also agree on the "emergency" advantage, even if the latter is a qualitative factor?

True interest rates of leases. Let us turn to a more complicated example of how illusory that quoted rate of interest can be. A client recently told me that his money worries were over. He had obtained for his customers all the financing needed from a well-known lessor at only 6% pre-tax! Lessor bought my client's energy-saving equipment from him for $300,000 per unit and leased each unit to a highly creditworthy end user. The lease rate was $60,000 per year ($300,000 spread equally over the five-year lease) plus 6% interest on the cost of $300,000, or $18,000 per year. The total annual lease rate was thus $78,000, payable quarterly in advance.

Other key factors:

1. Although technologically sophisticated, the equipment was very unlikely to become obsolete.

2. The $300,000 cost excluded a five-year warranty as to performance and maintenance over that period.

3. Hence at the end of five years the lessor would own a fully paid for and owned, readily salable unit in perfect operating condition, well-maintained, and worth at least 50% of its original price.

With these conditions established we can quantify the lessor's cash flows, assuming a 50% tax rate, for each quarter during which the lessor has an economic interest in the transaction. (These calculations are for discounted cash flow purposes only. Accounting records kept for financial reporting and tax purposes may differ significantly.)

It is clear from the table on page 170 that the lessor recovers substantially more by the end of this project than he laid out during it, $159,000 more, over the 5½ periods. But how can this be translated into a rate of interest? The answer is provided by a device called the present value calculation. All the flows of money are brought to the day of the closing at their discounted value as if they occurred at the moment of the closing (the same day as the signature of the documents and the availability of funds, we will assume). The discounting of the future payments becomes greater the further they take place into the future. Remember, a dollar received today is worth more than a dollar received tomorrow.

Through solution of a nonlinear algebraic equation we can do this—with the help of a computer—and arrive at the rate of interest for discounting the future payments to make them equivalent to the initial outlay.

Now refer in the table opposite to the 23rd Period, Cumulative Column, which shows a derived value of $0.001 thousand or just $1. This means that the computer has worked out the present value rate required to bring all cash flows, in and out, back to equality on day one (or near enough as makes no never-mind). That rate is 21.7%, after tax, and that rate, before overhead and risk, is what the lessor

```
          TABLE FOR IROR PROOF
          ---------------------------
```

PERIOD	CASHFLOW	PRESENT VALUE	CUMULATIVE
1	-280.500	-280.500	-280.500
2	19.500	18.567	-261.933
3	60.000	54.398	-207.535
4	21.000	18.129	-189.406
5	18.000	14.796	-174.610
6	18.000	14.088	-160.522
7	18.000	13.414	-147.108
8	18.000	12.773	-134.335
9	17.625	11.908	-122.426
10	17.625	11.339	-111.088
11	17.625	10.797	-100.291
12	17.625	10.280	-90.011
13	17.625	9.789	-80.222
14	17.625	9.320	-70.902
15	17.625	8.875	-62.027
16	17.625	8.450	-53.577
17	17.625	8.046	-45.531
18	17.625	7.661	-37.869
19	17.625	7.295	-30.574
20	17.625	6.946	-23.628
21	140.250	52.629	29.000
22	-9.750	-3.484	25.517
23	-75.000	-25.516	0.001

```
TABLE OF RATE OF RETURN VS. PRESENT VALUE
-------------------------------------------
```

NOMINAL ROR/YR %	TRUE ROR/YR %	PRESENT VALUE $
0.00	0.00	159.000
5.00	5.09	108.600
10.00	10.38	66.330
15.00	15.87	30.699
20.00	21.55	0.509
25.00	27.44	-25.206
30.00	33.55	-47.228

ALL FIGURES IN THOUSANDS OF DOLLARS

1st yr. Jul. 1 Lessor purchase of equipment (300.0)
2nd yr. Jan. 1 Lessor reduces his taxes 6 months from 1st yr
  July 1st with investment tax credit and energy tax credit 39.0

	Lease payments and residual value	Tax depreciation[a]	Taxable income	Ordinary income tax due (50%)	Cash tax effect[b]	Cash flow
1st yr. Jul 1	19.5	22.5	(3.0)	(1.5)	—	(280.5)[d]
Oct. 1	19.5	22.5	(3.0)	(1.5)	—	19.5
2nd yr. Jan. 1	19.5	16.5	3.0	1.5	(40.5)[c]	60.0
Apr. 1	19.5	16.5	3.0	1.5	(1.5)	21.0
Jul. 1	19.5	16.5	3.0	1.5	1.5	18.0
Oct. 1	19.5	16.5	3.0	1.5	1.5	18.0
3rd yr. Jan. 1	19.5	15.75	3.75	1.875	1.5	18.0
Apr. 1	19.5	15.75	3.75	1.875	1.5	18.0
Jul. 1	19.5	15.75	3.75	1.875	1.875	17.625
through	—	—	—	—	—	—
5th yr. Oct. 1	19.5	15.75	3.75	1.875	1.875	17.625
6th yr. Jan. 1	19.5	—	19.5	9.75	1.875	17.625
Apr. 1	19.5	—	19.5	9.75	1.875	17.625
Jul. 1	150.0	—	150.0	75.0	9.75	140.25
Oct. 1	—	—	—	—	9.75	(9.75)
7th yr. Jan. 1	—	—	—	—	75.00	(75.00)
Totals	540.0	300.0	240.0	120.0	81.0	159.0

[a]Not a cash event but required to determine tax liability
[b]Assume 6-month delay from book entries
[c]Includes ITC and ETC of $39.0
[d]$300 purchase of equipment less 1st Q lease payment in advance

expects to earn on the transaction. It is a far cry from the pre-tax of 6%, or an after-tax rate of 3%, that my client proudly announced.

Do not guess that by saying "before overhead and risk" I am throwing you a curve ball. *All* credit transactions entail overhead and risk. In the example chosen they should not affect the interest rate by more than three percentage points.

The client, by the way, was not wrong in the larger sense. His business was to manufacture and sell equipment at a profit, as much as possible. Since the lessor facilitated this primary goal and at the same time eliminated my client's need for more and more financing, his strategy was sound. Tactically, though, he could have negotiated a much better deal for himself and/or his ultimate customers if he had bothered to work out what a rich pudding he had handed over to the lessor.

An important part of the lessor's advantage in this example results from tax credits which may be changed or eliminated by future tax legislation. That is not the point. The point is that quoted "interest rates" are often not what they seem and may be grossly misleading, regardless of changes in the tax law.

This review cannot tell you everything about the techniques of calculating interest rates and comparing them. It *can* tell you that the more complicated the transaction, the more pitfalls there are, and the easier it is to accept simplistic or misleading numbers. Federal and state "truth-in-lending" laws are designed to protect consumers, that is, individual private borrowers. The business borrower must be his own watchdog. If your accountant is independent and his practice small, he may not be able to help you without much expensive research. (If he is not doing present value calculations fairly often, he will almost certainly consult a textbook to find the answer for you— something you could have done yourself.) A better and free source of guidance is probably one of the lenders you are negotiating with, as discussed earlier. An instructor in accounting or finance at a local college might be an excellent advisor for a reasonable fee.

Leases are particularly tricky since the tax advantages sometimes can be transferred between lessor and lessee, according to their advantages. A maintenance contract, if included in the lease rate, introduces another complication. For the small lease it may be impossible to determine what the financial consequences are to the lessee unless the equipment can also be purchased outright, e.g., a standard photocopier. In this case you can make a conventional rent vs. buy calculation and easily arrive at the rate of interest implicit in the lease.

As usual, the best way to ensure you are getting the best rate is to shop amongst several suppliers. When the leased value of the equipment is sizable, say over $100,000, you should ask to see the lessor's calculations of his financial return. He may balk at this or even give you fudged numbers, but it is worth a try. For much larger leases, you should *demand* to see the lessor's calculations. If he refuses, take your business elsewhere. Also, be alert to the possibility that the lessor may try to show you a very low rate of interest because he has built part of his financing profit into the assumed capital value of the asset to be leased. This is an old trick, and the only way to counter it is by getting competitive quotes on the asset itself, as if you were going to buy it outright.

A note of comfort. If the concept of present value and related esoterica leave you bewildered, do not be discouraged. Most people react the same way. I do myself, until with a bit of effort I refamiliarize myself with the subject.

A note of caution. Unless you plan to write a scholarly paper on the matter, do not get involved deeply in the theory of present value calculations. The potential complications are endless; they are analyzed and disputed in learned journals. They need concern only one investment decision in a thousand; and if you have that one in a thousand, you will know it. Otherwise, stick to the methodology illustrated earlier in this appendix.

In the event a present value calculation is warranted but for some reason you do not want to make it, try to force your potential suppliers of funds to quote against identical payment and other terms. This should force their different rates of interest to the surface. Bids that are not arithmetically and chronologically comparable may be worthless unless you are able to rearrange them to be comparable.

If you get into leasing at all deeply, the question of residual value often becomes critical. Residual value is what the asset you have leased will be worth at the end of the lease or, contractually, what the lease says it may be purchased for. The two values are not necessarily the same. The lease can entitle the lessee to acquire title to the asset for a nominal price (say, $1), for the then-market value, or for any other amount. In your eagerness to take possession of and put into use a new asset you may easily ignore the importance of this value which, after all, may be many years distant. Resist this temptation. The residual value may be extremely important in several different ways.

First, what you have to pay for it. Assume you have leased expensive, custom-built fixtures, furniture, and fittings for a luxury retail store. The term of the lease is four years. What price should you pay for these assets at the end of the lease? The answer is $1. Since the lessor knows that

1. removing the assets and reusing them elsewhere is not practical; and

2. he is most unlikely to find a successor at the same location who will want those same assets, his lease rate will include the full recovery to him of the cost of the assets. You will have paid for them in full, and the lessor will have depreciated them in full. If

you are still in business, they will probably be of much value to you, so ensure that the lease entitles you to buy them for $1. If the lessor refuses, then insist that the lease rate be reduced to reflect the future value the lessor places on them. The lessor is no fool: he will agree to $1.

Second, the effect on the lease rate. Suppose you want to lease a railway freight car for five years. At the end of that period, assuming proper maintenance, the wagon will still have a remaining useful life of 25 years. Your lease rate should reflect this high residual value: it should include a charge for depreciation of no more than a third of the value of the asset. (The lessor can easily move the wagon and lease it to new customers for another 25 years.) In this scenario there is no way the lessor will give you an option to buy the wagon for $1 at the end of the lease.

Third, the accounting treatment. The authority which sets the rules for accounting is the Financial Accounting Standards Board (FASB). Its ruling No. 13 covers the handling of leased assets. FASB 13 is an extremely complex document, its language impenetrable to the layman. When leasing assets of small value, such as a typewriter, ignore it. Large leases will have to abide by its mandates.

The gist of FASB 13 is that when the total present value of lease payments plus the present (estimated) residual value of the asset are significantly less than the capital cost of the asset, then the lease is classified as an *operating lease.* In your books you treat the lease payments no differently than you would monthly rentals for leased office space. If the total present values just referred to equal or exceed the capital cost of the asset, then it is considered a *capital lease;* and the asset must be shown on your balance sheet, together with the off-setting liability of the present value of the future lease payments. This accounting treatment must be observed no matter which party has legal title to the asset.

The purpose of FASB 13 is to force companies to show on their books assets that they are, in effect, buying, even though they do not have or never may take legal title to the assets. Now we come to the point of this discussion: if you must book a leased asset as a capital lease, then the additional debt on your balance sheet might seriously affect your creditworthiness, your image, and your borrowing power. Hence, before entering into any major lease, other than conventional real estate leases, you should explore these ramifications with your lessor, your accountant, and your banker.

Fourth, the tax treatment. This consideration is a real mine field, especially because the tax law has been changed, is changing, and will be changed in the future. I am sorry to say that if the amount is substantial, you really must consult an expert to avoid pitfalls and possibly to pick up some windfalls. If the lessor is a large, responsible company such as Greyhound Leasing, your account officer will probably be able to explain these effects. Smaller finance companies and lessors, too, usually have resident experts whose advice is free, as long as they smell some business. The key principle to keep in mind is that the tax treatment of the lease and its related assets and obligations is a major determinant of the amounts and timing of the cash flows; and these latter, as we have seen, are what determine your true rate of interest.

Insofar as any generalization is possible in the area of residual value, this is it: the residual value interacts with the lease rate; as one goes up, the other goes down. You cannot have it both ways. You can, however, determine which combination of high/low lease rate/residual value is to your benefit and then marshal arguments that the lessor's assumption of residual value is too high or too low. You may well be more knowledgeable than the lessor about the particular asset involved, and that may give you an edge in negotiations.

Did you notice that earlier in this appendix there was a trick? It was the 6% interest rate on the capital value of the $300,000 energy-saving equipment! This is the oldest scam in the history of leasing and installment purchases. The 6% "interest rate" was applied to the initial purchase value, not the time-weighted value of the principal not paid down. Since you pay down the principal of the loan throughout its life, the principal (or capital) payments have to be subtracted from the amount you owe to determine your true rate of interest.

The present value calculation we did exposed the speciousness of the 6%, as well as quantifying the effect of all the other advantages to the lessor.*

---

* I am grateful to Lockwood Rianhard, of Randolph, NJ, an expert in financial computation, who provided the computerized calculations for the energy-saving equipment lease.

APPENDIX D. ASSET-BASED LENDING AND BANKING REFERRALS

"Asset-based lending" is currently a popular phrase that appears to hold the promise of new credit where none was available before. Not really. Lenders have been advancing funds against the security of assets since Babylonian times, and what else is a home mortgage if not an asset-based loan?

To grasp the import of the phrase "asset-based lending" we must go back to an earlier era in American commercial lending, roughly the decades before 1965. That year marks approximately the time when adoption of the Uniform Commercial Code (UCC) became almost universal amongst the 50 states of the Union. Before then, state laws governing lenders' rights in collateral varied greatly, were archaic and complex, and usually did not provide commercial banks with convenient protection for their interests in collateralized assets. As a result, commercial banks generally did not collateralize their loans; they lent on an unsecured basis, depending on their analytical skills and experience to ensure repayment.

The lending criteria of the commercial banks, necessarily conservative under these circumstances, left huge numbers of businesses without access to commercial bank credit, so many of them turned to finance companies and factors for funds. These institutions had developed the specialized expertise required to lend successfully to less creditworthy businesses, using their assets as collateral. Although, because of the state of the law at that time, securing, monitoring, and seizing collateralized assets was complicated and expensive, still it was possible. These lenders had to charge much more for their services than the commercial banks, but the market for their money and skills was immense, and they grew in size and number.

Then the UCC arrived. Terminology, documentation, legal questions, rules of evidence, all were vastly simplified. The commercial

175

banks could have jumped into their competitors' markets, but banks, being banks, moved only slowly to exploit their new opportunities. Meanwhile, the factoring and finance houses expanded at an accelerating rate, for the same UCC drastically reduced *their* operating expenses and greatly increased the range and ease of collateralization. Historically they had the expertise to take advantage of the new law, and the commercial banks did not. In 1970 the volume of accounts receivable factored outside the commercial banks was $10 billion; in 1980 it was $29 billion.

Today the factors and commercial finance companies call themselves "asset-based lenders"; but if the quality of the borrower is adequate, they will make unsecured loans. At the same time, the commercial banks (the "non-asset-based" lenders) will require a lien on the assets of all but their most creditworthy customers. Hence the two finance sectors are converging, and perhaps a generation from now there will no longer be any perceptible distinction. Nevertheless, for the time being, the two sectors do tend to offer different products and to lend on different terms and conditions. These differences are very effectively summarized in the following tables which show the advantages and disadvantages of asset-based lending both from the borrower's and the lender's points of view.*

The table opposite demonstrates that the choice between an asset-based lender and a commercial bank can be a complicated one. Unless you investigate what each has to offer, you may not wind up with the credit best suited to your needs. Refer to Chapter 5, Selecting Target Lenders. For a free national listing of more than 225 asset-based lenders write to: National Commercial Finance Association, 225 West 34th Street, New York, NY, 10001.

By the way, if you contact one of these finance houses, and the loan officer says that your credit requirements are too small to meet its minimum, do the obvious: ask him for the names of two smaller, local finance companies that would be interested in your business. Underneath the larger asset-based lenders are many hundreds of well-run, medium-sized companies. Possibly they are in a position to give more attention to a small credit than a big firm could. Further, if a big-name

---

* Used with the kind permission of Doreen A. Wolchik, an executive with a major finance house. The tables are adapted from her article in the November, 1984, issue of the *National Commercial Finance Association Journal.* I have also drawn background from her article for my historical sketch of the industry.

Borrower's Point of View

Advantages

- Open-ended financing. There is no regular repayment schedule as long as the collateral can support the outstanding loan.
- No compensating balance required. Interest is paid only on funds borrowed.
- Higher total borrowing capacity. Normally more can be borrowed on a secured than an unsecured basis. Credit limit based on the borrower's collateral, not his net worth.
- More flexible. As the business and assets grow, the availability of credit grows.
- Probably cheaper than raising equity, if that is the only alternative.
- Sometimes invaluable in leveraged buy-outs, acquisitions, and other extraordinary situations.

Disadvantages

- Interest rate usually higher than conventional borrowing.
- Lender requires current and detailed reports, often daily, e.g., sales assignments, remittance reports.
- Other creditors may look askance at liens on most or all of available assets.
- Some trade creditors still view asset-based lending as a sign of financial instability.

Lender's Point of View

Advantages

- Attractive pricing. The riskier and more complex the deal, the higher the rate charged.
- In case of bankruptcy collateral is secured.
- Ability to monitor and control company's daily flow of cash and progress.
- Loan is always on a demand basis, so advances are discretionary, based on the account manager's current appraisal of risk.
- Opens the door for creative financing.

Disadvantages

- Administratively expensive due to strict controls to monitor collateral.
- High-risk customers could result in costly workouts or liquidation.
- Highly competitive market.
- Shortage of experienced personnel to administer this type of credit.

lender recommends a smaller competitor, almost certainly the latter will be a reputable firm, not a fly-by-night usurer. This is better than picking names at random from the Yellow Pages.

Most lenders, including commercial banks, have referral networks. The larger ones routinely refer small applicants to smaller institutions (assuming they do not offer a full range of services), and small lenders will refer an applicant for a very large credit to an institution they think will be interested. These are generally not "put-offs." On the contrary, they are usually valuable guides into the right door.

Size alone may not be the obstacle. Your local commercial bank may know nothing about export financing, perhaps too small a market to warrant hiring a resident specialist. Chances are it *will* know another bank which would love to have your business. If your contact does not volunteer an alternative lender, you have to ask, ask, and ask again. *Somebody* in that institution knows where to find what you want: otherwise it would have died years ago from arteriosclerosis. [Probably, though I've seen some wondrous examples of the living dead.]

APPENDIX E. BREAKEVEN ANALYSIS

One of the simplest and most useful tools for analyzing investments and describing them to investors and lenders, is the breakeven analysis. As its name suggests, its purpose is to determine what minimum level of sales is required for a project to break even, that is, to begin to show a profit. It is also called a payout calculation. In the following example, I call it "Recovery of Investment." As long as you have your concepts and mechanics straight, it usually does not matter what you call it: any reasonably experienced business or financial reader will see exactly what you are shooting for.

I obtained this example directly from a prospectus I prepared for a client who was soliciting equity investors to finance the completion of an animated cartoon on alcohol abuse. In this case production of the film was well advanced, and the cost to complete it could be estimated accurately, as could be the later, variable expenses of reproduction, marketing, and so forth. The arithmetic is shown in the tables beneath the graph; the graph itself is merely a convenient and effective way of visualizing the numbers. It shows that the fixed or "sunk" investment by the outside investors can be recovered from the sale of only 1,767 prints. Sales above that number will produce a healthy gross margin, and that margin will go right down to the bottom line (before taxes, but no income taxes are payable on the recovery of the investment). Since total sales projected, on the basis of a marketing study, were only 8,000 copies, the potential investor could quickly see that even if the enterprise sold only 22% of forecast sales, at least he would get his money back.

The outside investors would have first call on the net cash inflow until their capital was repaid. Everything beyond that was gravy. The graph does not go into the formulae for division of profits after the outside investors are repaid, since the point of the graph was to simplify a presentation of the investors' risk as regards the forecast volume of sales.

179

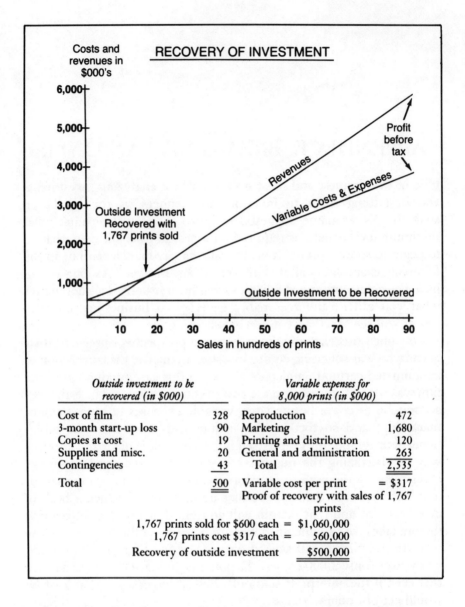

Conveniently, the example above happens to be a simple one, though it is nonetheless realistic. If the success of your own project depends heavily on sales volume, some such breakeven analysis will help you and your lender to grasp more easily the risks and margins of error. Once you understand the arithmetic of the example here, you can adjust this model to suit your own project and conditions.

APPENDIX F. SOURCES OF GOVERNMENTAL ASSISTANCE

The United States Small Business Administration (SBA) has several programs to assist the small business enterprise, whether just getting started or seeking to expand. The SBA definition of "small," and therefore eligible for SBA assistance is 1) net worth does not exceed $6 million; and 2) average net income after tax for the preceding two years was not more than $2 million. More than 98 out of a 100 firms will meet these criteria, and those which don't might qualify under other standards. The telephone directory of the nearest large town or city will give you an SBA number to call.

The SBA has been subject to severe cuts in budgetary appropriations during the past few years, and there are powerful political forces that seek to demolish it completely. Hence I'm reluctant to devote much space to programs that may be curtailed or even abolished. Suffice it to say that in the past the SBA has helped provide loan financing to tens of thousands of small businesses which could not by themselves obtain credit from the private markets. As far as credit is concerned, it should not be your first port of call: its requirements are cumbersome and its procedures rigid and time-consuming. However, if at least two commercial banks reject your applications, you should take these refusals (in writing) to the SBA and see whether it is prepared to step in with guarantees or direct advances. Businesses owned by minorities, the handicapped, and women may find themselves especially favored.

In addition to its programs of credit assistance, the SBA has many excellent publications designed to educate and assist the small firm. You can obtain a free catalogue of them from your regional SBA office.

The SBA has a less well-known program: free consulting services called SCORE (Service Corps of Retired Executives). On your request the SBA will scan its register of retired businessmen in your area for those who can best advise you on specific problems. It will arrange for them to give you the benefit of their experience and judgment. On the whole these experts are definitely *not* senile fuddy-duddies with nothing better to do. They are recently retired successful executives, full of savvy, and their time is free. This resource should never be neglected by firms too small to hire specialist staff or professional consultants.

All state governments have departments to encourage commerce and industry. Their programs range from issuing worthless propaganda to loans at subsidized rates of interest, pools of venture capital, valuable tax concessions, and even outright grants for physical plant, relocation, and training. These programs are too diverse and mutable to cover here. Any entrepreneur whose project holds forth the promise of more than a few jobs should investigate them, especially if it is the kind of business governments like: high technology manufacturing, low-tech manufacturing in areas of high unemployment, research, high-tech service industries, or low-tech service industries in the right place (e.g, a luxury restaurant on a decaying waterfront area scheduled for redevelopment).

It is a wonder how generously some of these state agencies will hand out money, though not so wondrous when you consider that the jobs of the people who hand out the money depend on their constantly dispensing it. Ferret through the names of the organizations in your target state: Economic Development Agency, Industrial Loan Fund, Commercial Enterprise Board. These outfits may have big bucks to hand out. Many of them have more money than common sense or candidates to borrow it or give it to.

I don't like it; probably you don't like it. But since the Reagan administration stopped filling many of the troughs from Washington, some states have launched their own gravy boats. Applications to these agencies for assistance, unlike applications to a bank, should promise the world. This is how John DeLorean coaxed scores of millions of pounds from the North Ireland Development Board, and it is not all that different over here.

If you have the flexibility as to location, play the economic incentives offered by one state off against those offered by another. It becomes no different than bargaining with several suppliers. Get offers from two or three different states; then lead them into a Dutch auction to obtain the most lucrative deal.

Never rely on these incentives to make a success of your business, however attractive they are. If the basic economics are not sound, no amount of governmental subsidy will create an enduring, profitable enterprise. The numbers may look too good to resist, but *please* believe me: governmental subsidies, contracts, protection, concessions, grants, whatever, will fail to keep alive a business which does not have a firm economic foundation in the free market.

I'm not moralizing or preaching capitalist economic philosophy. I'm just telling you the results of my experience, which covers three decades, many different industries, and a lot of geography. Proving out my argument would require too many stories, some of them embarrassing to me and, though we acted in good faith, to the governmental agencies with whom I negotiated.

City, county, and other local agencies below the state level may sometimes offer incentives to a new employer/investor or even inducements to stay put. Governments can help in other surprising ways. A client of mine in Newark, New Jersey, discovered that, in the desolation surrounding him, he was able to have his warehouse declared a protected, historical building. With that certification in hand he was able to protect his economic interests not only in his warehouse, but in the surrounding acreage, an area ripe for redevelopment.

If you do not look for such opportunities, you will never discover what our several levels of government have to offer. There is no secret information I can give you here; but if you have the determination, you may uncover treasures. Long after I had given up, clients of mine have done it. You can, too.

Here's an example that arrived in my mail just while finishing this book:

> *The Liberty Circle fund was recently created to invest in start-up and early stage companies located in (or willing to relocate to) the area within a twenty-five mile radius of the Statue of Liberty. The fund has been initially capitalized with $10 million by the Port Authority of New York and New Jersey but will expand to include other major corporate limited partners.*
>
> *[The Fund] invests in such areas as biotechnology and pharmaceuticals, graphic arts, communications, retailing, apparel, and health care as well as companies whose products and services address the area's huge base of financial institutions.*

In this case the specific investments will be selected and managed by Adler & Co., a private venture capital firm, so the investment criteria will be more hard-nosed than those of a typical governmental fund. No matter. Suddenly here is a source of finance where before there was none!

Index